W9-BWL-020

HARDBALL JOB HUNTING TACTICS

HARDBALL JOB HUNTING TACTICS

DICK WRIGHT

A Work In America Institute Book

Facts On File Publications
460 Park Avenue South
New York, N.Y. 10016

This book is dedicated to:

Jan Bourdon—for her brains and loyalty—ditto for Angie Raub
Dick Cooper for his friendship
Michael Rosow for his faith
Wilma Wright Hamblen for her love and influence on my life.

HARDBALL JOB HUNTING TACTICS

Dick Wright

Published by Facts On File, Inc.
460 Park Avenue South, New York, N.Y. 10016

Library of Congress Cataloging in Publication Data

Wright, Dick.
Hardball job hunting tactics.

1. Job hunting. I. Title.
HF5382.7.W74 1982 650.1'4 82-18357
ISBN 0-87196-134-2

Printed in the United States of America
10 9 8 7 6 5 4 3 2 1

CONTENTS

Work in America Institute wishes to acknowledge its appreciation to the Exxon Education Foundation for providing the funds necessary to undertake the research and writing of this book.

The statements made and views expressed herein are those of the author and do not necessarily reflect the views of the Exxon Education Foundation.

FOREWORD

WHY I BELIEVE MY BOOK CAN HELP YOU

Looking for a job is one of life's most painful experiences. The roadblocks to hiring set up by business and industry to ensure that those hired meet the employer's needs for productivity and efficiency can be and are sources of a demoralizing loss of personal self-esteem. The effect of this loss of self-esteem can range from a temporary setback to a permanent halt in personal vocational progress. From the point of view of business and industry, this emphasis on productivity and efficiency is understandable; for a job-seeker, however, rejection can be devastating. This book is designed to minimize the rejection factor and maximize the job-acceptance factor.

There are many good job-search books. Most address specific problems but often fail to provide a complete approach to competitive job-seeking; they do not address the trauma and feelings of isolation that can and usually do accompany a job search. The ingredients missing include up-to-date knowledge of what employers want to see and hear at every step of the hiring process and an understanding of today's more sophisticated hiring practices.

This book does not soften its message to you, and it covers the very problems many job-search books skirt. You will find straight answers that will clear most roadblocks to obtaining a job and a lot of advice on improving your current hirability and future career advancement.

This book will teach you what employers expect from an applicant and how you can fulfill those expectations. It's a four-step process, divided into four easy-to-understand and easy-to-follow sections that will enable you to put your best foot forward and get the job offers—and the job—you want.

Section One: "Getting You Ready" will show you how to create an Employment Package. We won't trap you or force you into becoming something you can't handle easily in terms of your personality or education. Relax. When you complete the preparation section you will have an Employment Package, which consists of a cover letter, application for employment and a resume or personal profile.

Handling these three steps correctly will get you the interview, and we will furnish interview questions and answers and advise what attitude you should have during the interview. (How often have you said to yourself, "If I could just get the interview, I know I could get the job!"?)

Finally, we'll teach you how to compose the all-important *thank-you letter,* which will wipe out half your competition.

Section Two: "Where and How to Look for a Job" will teach you how to look for or apply for a job without having to leave your home. All you need is a telephone, postage, paper and envelopes. Anyone can tap the hidden job market with our methods so long as they can be understood on the phone and can read at an eighth-grade level. If you do not have a telephone and have no choice but to apply in person, at least you will know what you submitted is solid, with a better-than-average chance to be read favorably. Your chances for acceptance will increase automatically.

Since roughly 70 percent of the job-opening market is "hidden"—not advertised—we will teach you how to get into the departments where the jobs are open, interview without completing the screening formalities first and discover where the decision to hire is made. Then all the personnel department has to do is check your references, report "no problem" to the hiring, decision-making department head and sign you up.

For those jobs that are advertised, we will show you how to reply properly to want ads by telephone or by mail. We will tell you how to be so well prepared when you approach employment agencies that they will consider you for employer-pays-the-fee jobs.

Section Three: "The Right Way to Change Jobs" will teach you how and when to change jobs successfully. There's a right way and a wrong way to change jobs, and a right time and a wrong time to make the move. There are solid tips in this section so you'll never have to worry about what your past employer will say about you if you leave, and we also tell you how to impress your new employer when you take the job he or she offers you.

Section Four: "Advice to the Hard-to-Employ" tackles the problem of people who have been often unfairly labeled as the hard-to-employ: offenders and ex-offenders, single parents, black youth, the handicapped, the work-injured, ex-CETA employees, and others. There are ways to present yourself effectively despite tough breaks in your past or just not being lucky enough to be born a perfectly desirable employee. My book shows you all the angles you can play that will put you on the road to success.

Before you go any farther in my book, I think you should know who I am and something about how my techniques were developed.

Previous business experience with such firms as Ford Motor Company, Renault-Peugeot, 3M, Rockwell, a division of King Resources, and decision-making positions in the area of sales, marketing, administration, accounting, research/development, purchasing, customer service, and personnel prepared to mount a self-directed job-search program. For the past ten years, I have gained extensive knowledge and experience in human services, including nationwide support programs relating to the employment of CETA clients.

When I combined my actual business experience with human services experience, it did not take long for me to conclude that human service employment programs—for all of their good intentions in helping others—were missing two prime ingredients for success: (1) most did not have the ability to provide a final "link" to their services, that of actual transition into business-for-profit jobs, and (2) they failed to eliminate a dependency factor so people could get or change jobs on their own.

I looked at what other "self-directed job search programs" were attempting and decided to design a program combining basic components required for any job search *but* also creating a supportive but "no nonsense" approach that could be applied simultaneously to people at all levels of education as well as to those with socioeconomic problems. This meant a minimum of "counseling" on past problems [avoiding the "armchair psychiatrist" approach and hand-holding] and getting and *sticking* to the point: job-search techniques to meet employer expectations for a desirable applicant and catering to employer hiring practices. Because of the volume of people who went through our workshop—some 1,700 in three years—my staff was chosen on the basis of their knowledge of business as well as of human services and for their ability to stick to the no-nonsense approach without spending the majority of their time in individual counseling. We did not use a hit-or-miss approach. As word spread of our techniques and successes, specialized agencies dealing in the hard-to-employ, such as current and ex-offenders, blacks, former CETA employees, blue-collar men and women, senior citizens, the work-injured, and displaced homemakers, sought to enter their clients into our program.

While we cannot place all those who buy this book into an actual workshop setting, you are receiving the same basic techniques, both for preparation and actual job search, that have been used to get jobs for an average of 73 percent of those who attended our workshops.

I believe every answer for practically every hiring problem is covered here. You are about to learn how employers think about and react to people who apply to them for jobs. This is not a book for those with extreme problems only. This book will assist anyone looking for a job, regardless of educational level or employment history. You cannot find a job-search program that gives every technique we have provided here. Our technique is not taught in schools, nor is self-directed job search commonly available throughout the country in human-services employment programs, even though there is great potential for blending self-directed placement methods with traditional job development and placement. Such a program would give employers a worker with a constructive *attitude* as well as a skill, at the same time avoiding deadending participants who have heretofore relied on dependency-factor programs for employment.

Following the exposure of countless people to our program and a two-year tour of Department of Labor-sponsored Job Development Workshops developed by the Work in America Institute, Inc., it has been generally agreed that the methods used by our organization and others like it seem to be the wave of the future.

We hope you will enjoy this book as much as the participants in my Job Search Workshops. I promise you that my advice is easy to follow, is written in plain English and, above all, is practical: It works in the best way possible—it will get you work. There is something for everybody in this book and everything for many. Most importantly, I think you'll find what *you* are looking for.

Good job-hunting. Remember, tomorrow is the first day of your new career.

Dick Wright

INTRODUCTION

IS THIS BOOK FOR YOU?

ATTENTION: JOB SEEKER AND JOB GIVER

This book *is* for you if you've been rejected for a job or if you do not know how to go about finding one. It features special answers and advice for the so-called hard-core unemployed or underemployed such as ex-offenders, single parents, welfare recipients, black teens, Hispanics and other minorities. And this book is also for people in industry, who will discover why they've missed out on having the services of a lot of good employees by practicing hiring overkill, and how they can attract and employ the best candidates for the jobs they offer.

READ THIS, OR DON'T READ THE REST OF THE BOOK

In the past four years, the Job Search Workshops program has served over 2,500 clients considered extremely hard to employ. That term might indicate that these people were hard to employ because they did *not* want to work. But we found that 73 percent of our clients went to work on their own once they were shown how. Why had these job hunters failed in the past? No one had told them how to be effective in getting work, and they were unprepared to deal with stiff and sophisticated hiring practices. It's easy to see why they found the process baffling and traumatic; after all, for them hunting for a job meant one rejection after another. You will see the word "rejection" a lot in this book; in 80 percent of our cases, clients were previously rejected for jobs through no fault of their own.

Getting a job and doing a job are two different things. Getting a job is a challenge. We will demonstrate to you in this book how to meet that challenge by showing you how to get your act together without asking you to do a lot of boring exercises. Other job-search books give you that; this one gives you a step-by-step plan to landing a job, and it works in the most practical way: It will put *you* to work.

Our methods will be presented in simple terms; you will be able to use these methods immediately. In general, we will address our answers and explanations to those with very few past problems, but we will also give special attention to those with lots of past problems. We will tell you how to compete for a job without constant rejection; deal with rebuilding from your past mistakes in several different ways; and cover a number of special personal and social handicaps. In the Job Search Workshops we have dealt more in specifics than in generalizations, and we write out of our experience in applying these specifics to real-life situations and working with hard-to-employ job seekers.

Our theory is simple. Too many people have experienced personal agony looking for work and participating in social-service programs that did not help them. These people, skilled and unskilled, usually have suffered rejection from business and industry that has left them bewildered about the American Dream. They have been willing to work to achieve a decent living standard, only to be rejected . . . simply because no one taught them how to meet employer expectations.

A WORD *ABOUT* EMPLOYERS—AND *TO* THEM

As most of you already know, many employers are decent people. They take care of their employees, pay them for good work and promote them. More and more American employers are realizing that the treatment of their workers means the difference between high productivity and lagging results. These employers know and understand the value of psychologically and financially rewarding their employees, thereby improving productivity and profit so that everyone wins and nobody loses.

But some employers are not so good. In fact, some treat their employees very badly. Since you cannot change your employer's personality, you must be able to recognize a bad situation and change your job before you become a victim. Unfortunately, one cannot always identify a bad employer until it is too late. By that time you may have been made to look like a failure instead of blame being shared by the employer. Using the lessons found in this book, you will be able to escape such employers in a professional manner *before* you are fired.

As for *your* attitude, you must realize that employers do not hire people who, on paper and in person, indicate that they would not contribute to productivity and profit. Some of these screening methods are justified, and a lot of them are overkill. They weed out a lot of good applicants along with high-risk candidates.

From the point of view of business and industry, employers are entitled to take this approach—it is *their* business, not yours. But it is up to employers, once you are hired, to make you feel that you are part of their business. Too many do not. That is why, in this book, we will tell you how to leave employers who do not do their part for you before your work experience becomes a nightmare for you and for them.

A WORD ABOUT YOUR ATTITUDE

If you refuse to follow the directions we give you, then you are either too stubborn to heed our advice or do not want to work. We found that about 15 to 18 percent of our clients did not really want to work, so we told them to come back when they felt they were ready; we say the same to you. If you are a job seeker, with or without skills, and sincerely want to work, then this book will give you what you need.

THREE GREAT EXPECTATIONS THIS BOOK WON'T FULFILL

1. *This is not a "career" book.* We cannot slot you into the exact work for your skills and provide eternal vocational bliss. This is a *survival* book and will give you more than an even break in getting work.
2. *We are not psychologists.* This book won't analyze and cure your deep-seated psychological problems. It will help you establish a better job-related self-image.
3. *We are not social authorities.* We're not going to pass moral judgments on you; that's the business of the courts and the church of your choice.

But we do know how to approach employers from *their* viewpoint, and we know what they expect in a desirable applicant. We are going to reveal to you the secrets of how they hire. We are not concerned with your past mistakes. We *do* care about telling you how to correct them, in order to start over, by giving you the answers you need and a new perspective about getting hired.

A WORD ABOUT YOUR PAST

Let's face it. Some of you have really blown it in past jobs. You have done things—as a result of boredom, pure laziness, resentment or other reasons—that come back to haunt you again and again when seeking a new job. Some of you have quit without notice, leaving an employer infuriated with you. Afterward you may say, "Am I glad *that's* over." But it's not over. Even if you are lucky enough to make it through an application and interview when you look for your next job, you are not hired. Why? Because an employer does—and MAKE NO MISTAKE ABOUT THIS—an employer does always check your references. The chances of your getting by one (or more) past mistakes are remote—unless you rebuild some of the bridges you burned.

Employers have made mistakes in the past, too, when they hired people who did not turn out to be good employees. So they are extremely cautious—so cautious that people who have nothing to conceal are examined just as closely as those who do. Moreover, there are so many applicants, for almost any job, that employers do not have to bother with anyone not demonstrating the personal presentation and attitudes they seek. *Anything* that might be a problem can cause you to be rejected. And they don't tell you why. They don't have to.

Some of you have attempted to cover gaps in employment, arrest records, dismissal from previous jobs and incomplete education. As you keep making changes, your application or resume becomes a tangle of lies and half truths. We will teach you how to eliminate problems or render them harmless and give yourself an even break. For all of you—with problems or without—this book teaches you how to dazzle an employer throughout the hiring process and get an offer of employment. You can display this dazzle, no matter what your education, as long as you are realistic about your skills, or about your ability to learn a skill at entry level. We teach you to be job *getters.*

We are going to teach you how to go after an *offer*—not a job—and why this attitude makes a difference to an employer and to you.

What is that difference? We're talking about being a seeker after offers of many possible jobs, from which you will choose the one that's right for you. It cuts down your feeling of desperation, your hunger to take a job, any job. That desperation is something an employer can sense—just the way a dog can sense fear in a frightened human. Once the employer senses that fear your chances for proper pay, working conditions, training and advancement are diminished; the employer knows you're in no position to bargain. He knows you'll take any job you can get. But when you are looking for offers, not jobs, you come across as a person with self-confidence, as someone who knows his or her own worth and who is not ready to work under whatever conditions are offered by the first job that turns up. Looking for offers allows you to keep your self-respect and personal dignity, and it ups your chances for landing the right job when it comes along. The potential employer feels obligated to make the job more attractive when he knows you may *not* accept his offer—providing, of course, he wants you to work for him to begin with.

With that approach you can use this book for the rest of your life without its methods becoming dated and, in doing so, you will also be doing business and industry a favor. We will unravel the confusion and tangled statements about your background in a way you can live with and that will make sense to any employer. Keep this bit of sage advice in mind at all times, especially when you feel down and out:

> IT IS NOT HE OR SHE WHO CAN NECESSARILY *DO THE JOB BEST* WHO IS HIRED, IT IS HE OR SHE WHO *KNOWS THE MOST ABOUT GETTING HIRED* WHO GETS THE JOB. (*Quest* magazine, 1980)

YOUR COMPETITION

Don't think that just because you discovered or applied for a job opening, you are going to be the only applicant. There will be *lots* of applicants. You will never see most of them, unless you are all sitting together in a waiting room, which is unlikely. Employers receive applications, read them and reject most of them at that stage. Next, they invite selected people for interviews and let them screen *themselves* out. From the remaining choices they check references, weigh all factors and then make the offer to *one* person. There is no second or third place in job-seeking. "Coming close" does not count—that makes you feel worse, if they bother to tell you. And they usually don't bother; you just sit by the phone, waiting for it to ring. And it doesn't.

If you follow the process for job-seeking that we give you in this book, you will reduce your chance of rejection and eliminate the competition as well. If you are unrealistic in seeking highly skilled work and do not have the skills to compete against those who do have them, then nothing can help you unless the employer is willing to train you. In that case, the procedures in this book will help you. The basic idea is to create a *primary* job objective. Then find where you stand with the skills you think you have for your primary job choice. And also find out who your competition is. *Find out.* We will show you the means to get through the doorway. Face the truth, *but* have a secondary goal or survival job in mind with skills you *know* you have for something you can and *will* do while you are getting the training to do the job you would rather do, or the primary goal. That way you won't be frustrated because you can't get what you want now. And that's all the "career" advice you'll get in this book. It all boils down, in the real world of the job marketplace, to being able to survive and be a "have" instead of a "have-not" until you can be a "have more." When you have what you need to go after a bigger, better job, pick up this book again. It'll be just as much help to you then as it was the first time you used it.

DEALING WITH REJECTION

Rejection is a word we use a lot in this book. The emotions of rejection are, among others: anger, fear, panic, anguish, isolation, frustration. They all create a loss of self-esteem, a low opinion of yourself and your abilities. Nowhere else in life (except perhaps in love) does rejection devastate self-esteem as much as in job-hunting. KEEP YOUR WITS! If you give in to the emotions of rejection, your competition wins the job while you're drowning in self-pity. Even if you follow our instructions, there will be *some* rejection. Some circumstances cannot be covered and corrected on paper. One of them is personal chemistry. No matter how well you present yourself, at any job-seeking stage, or how qualified you are, the person who hires can be adversely affected by your personal chemistry. This problem is almost unavoidable and is hard to measure and prevent. It just happens. (Personal chemistry can also be positive: You can be interviewed by someone who obviously "takes to you.")

The chemical reaction a decision maker has about you is not always in the best interest of the business or industry for whom the hirer works, but it *is* in his best interest if he's the person who must work with *you*. It does happen, but if you do as we suggest, you will know it was that and not something else.

The Employment Package we will show you how to create reduces your chances of rejection and keeps an employer from being supersensitive about you during the selection process by reacting to chemical stimuli—real or imagined—that can cause you to be eliminated. This happens most often at the interview when you can't back up what you wrote on your application and/or resume.

DO NOT LIVE IN MORTAL FEAR OF PERSONNEL DEPARTMENTS

Personnel departments must send properly skilled applicants (or at least applicants who have the right attitude to be trained for the job) to the department where the job is open and where the final decision to hire is made. If they send poorly prepared applicants, they come under fire from these departments, which must meet production quotas and deadlines. These departments work together to improve the productivity and efficiency of the company. That is what personnel departments must keep in mind at all times, and so should you.

The personnel department depends on the job description from a department with a job opening. In communication with that department's manager, the personnel department determines the skill level needed, and then candidates are selected to be interviewed by the department manager. The process they use is called the selection process. Since only one person is selected from among those interviewed, and the rest are not, this may seem, from your point of view, more like a rejection process, with all the misery that the word implies. After the selection process comes the screening process—and they do screen.

In all fairness, many interviewers are courteous; they understand the nervousness that comes with a job search and attempt to make the applicant comfortable. On the other hand (and this is something most of you can identify with), others are much less understanding. In fact, they are stern and unbending in the presence of an applicant and act as though they are "guardians of the gates." If you are ultimately rejected by such an interviewer, your self-esteem is usually damaged and you may be even more nervous the next time you are interviewed. But take heart!

First of all, don't judge a company solely by one or two people in its personnel department—it may still be a fine place to work. Second, the presentation methods we teach here will offset most of the effects of such a harsh approach, even in the worst cases. If you make your presentation as we tell you to and you still get a stern reception, don't react—keep trying with the tools we give you. Your goal is to get an interview with the person who makes the hiring decision and, ultimately, to receive a job offer.

Many businesses do not have a formal personnel department. If not, the same experiences can happen with the person directly responsible for hiring. Keep your dignity as a human being and walk out if necessary to keep it. If you give in to pressure hiring, you are only setting yourself up to experience pressure on the job and ultimate rejection. If you get by a tough hiring type, look to see if the rest of the company seems that way too. If they are, and you are hired and accept out of desperation to have a job, any job, you will not exactly find vocational heaven. That is why, again, we are going to teach you to go for an *offer,* not a job. Lots of offers.

SECTION ONE

GETTING YOU READY

A. LET'S GET THAT WORD "OVERQUALIFIED" OUT OF THE WAY FIRST

You have a skill or occupation composed of many smaller skills that contribute toward the title of your primary occupation. No job is available with that specific "title," so you try for a job utilizing one or more of the skills that make up the title—and you are told that you are "overqualified"! Because you need a job so desperately, being overqualified does not seem like a good reason, from *your point of view,* NOT to be hired. Because you forget to look at this decision from the employer's point of view, you suffer from rejection and experience a loss of self-esteem.

1. HERE'S WHY YOU WERE TOLD YOU WERE OVERQUALIFIED AND WERE REJECTED

The firm to which you are applying...

1. Worries about your ability to perform in a "lesser" position than you have held and the effect it will eventually have on your work.
2. Knows that you will expect quick promotion because of your other skills and that they cannot promote you fast enough to make you happy.
3. Knows that because of (2), as soon as a job meeting all the skills in your previous title becomes available somewhere else, you are likely to leave them. There goes their dollar investment in your training to be a productive employee for them, and they have to start again. They've taken a loss on you.

Because your resume is specific about your job objective and leaves no room for "related" job titles, you are screened out as overqualified. You are asking a company, simply by stuffing a resume into an envelope or completing an application for employment, to "read into" your skills and employ you because you are not only qualified for the job but have additional skills as well. You are not only OVERQUALIFIED, but your COMPETITION WILL EAT YOU ALIVE. There will be applicants for the job you want with a background that is absolutely right for the specific job opening, while you have only vague and related skills.

Don't get us wrong—you *can* get those jobs. You will not only have to match but also surpass your competition *at every turn* of the hiring process to do it. You need tools to tear the screener's eyes away from your background which, seemingly, has very little to do with their job that you need so desperately. This book will give you the tools to compete.

B. HOW TO FILL OUT THE APPLICATION

There are many types of application forms. Some are epics of design and complexity and immediately discourage job seekers. Large companies have been forced to make their application forms conform to laws such as those for equal employment opportunity and affirmative action. The forms can be long or short, depending on how much information they think they need the kinds of questions they ask. Small and medium-size companies may still be using old "illegal" forms because they are not monitored as closely by the government. Many, however, use standard forms, in pads, from stationery stores, and these forms are simple. Deceptively simple. They can still be used to screen you *out.* One thing is certain: some questions that can no longer be asked legally have been rephrased so that they are acceptable under the law—and still reveal everything companies want to know about you. (And, after all is said and done, companies still will check your references to make sure of their choice.)

Because of this, we have constructed an application form that asks many obvious questions, those with hidden meanings and those that are illegal. We do this to prepare you for any situation, written or verbal, that can trip you up. Other types of questions will be covered in the interview portion of this section.

We will provide the correct answers and tell you why they ask the questions, as well as address special problem solutions, by category for each question, so that you will know how they are used for screening out at this stage.

If you see questions on an application that you know are wrong or illegal, just answer them, using our answers. If you are filling it out in an employment office (you will learn you should not be doing this—if you follow our methods) *do not* stand up and scream: "YOU CAN'T ASK THIS!!!" If you do, you may experience instant self-gratification, but it is all over for you there and then. Instead of reacting, grit your teeth and answer the question. If you are still upset about this, then after you receive the offer and are hired, report the company to the U.S. Labor Department *anonymously.* They will clean up their act; you have a job, and a good feeling that you have protected others from illegal hiring processes. *Play their game while playing yours.* The same goes when you do not want to answer a question, can't answer a question or skip over a question. Leaving a blank in an obvious place, in which there is no excuse for not answering, will signal the screener that you are hiding something, being a nonconformist (the last thing they want or need) or are just plain sloppy about details.

Twenty-five hundred people have gone through our course just about as we present it here. It's incredible how many of those people—educated or not—considered an application for employment as "something to get over with" so they could "get on" with the interview. In other words, they thought they would receive an interview...period, and found an application to be a minor annoyance.

WRONG! Sometimes you have an interview; usually you do not at the application stage. In small companies, maybe; in big companies, rarely or never. Generally, you must wait until the employer has received all the applications they want during the recruiting process. If they like what they read on your application, you will be selected to come back. Therefore, the application is absolutely critical to your being granted an interview.

Do not cut corners on what we teach you about completing applications here. You must make each application *count.*

Follow our instructions and you will avoid a war of nerves in job-seeking. Do not consider any item or step as unimportant to your total approach. Personnel people, or anyone else in a business or industry, are not used to seeing the perfection you are going to achieve. We call it the "dazzle factor." You must dazzle them. If you do, and you are only *marginally* qualified for the job, they will not be able to resist seeing you and may even consider you for another position if you lose out on the one that is open, OR EVEN MAKE ROOM FOR YOU. The presentation we teach cannot be overlooked by any company skilled in recruiting because they seldom see one with such a professional approach. Personnel departments will have to give you the benefit of the doubt and take a look at you *if* you are qualified.

In small to medium-sized companies, the persons who do the screening can include owners, department heads, office managers and even lower-level employees. That is even better for your presentation because it is read by someone where the work is to be done. They are more apt to hire you from your presentation, to "give you a chance." AFTER ALL, YOU WILL BE GIVING THEM WHAT THEY WANT TO SEE AND HEAR! Even if the company has a personnel department, it will be delighted the manager picked his or her own employee.

As for formal personnel departments, you should remember that they are expected to screen out all but the most qualified candidates. And they are carefully trained to do so.

We know of three large-scale seminars to be held in three major California cities on the subject "Interviewing and Selecting Employees Today." The list of companies that have attended previous, similar seminars reads like a business and industry "Who's Who." Some of the topics are:

Why selection is the most important management decision.
How selection directly affects profit.
Avoid these seven costly mistakes in employee selection.
How you should prepare to interview an applicant.
How to read an application.
The eight-step approach to conducting a selection interview.
The best way to develop key data from the interview.
Three major strategies for gathering applicant data.
Tips on making reference checks pay off.

These are just a few of the topics, but they should give you some idea of how personnel departments operate.

The application form in this book is divided into three parts. Don't go on until you have completed each part. Part 1 deals with hidden-meaning questions that might be asked on an application or in an interview, exactly as we state them here or thinly disguised. Certain answers to those questions can screen you out and keep them from reading further, no matter what your skill level. Part 2 deals with your educational background, and Part 3 with your employment history. All three have only one thing in common: the need for dazzling detail. Remember: (1) The screeners do not know who you are, (2) they have not seen you, and (3) you are only "words on a piece of paper." But those words will determine if you are going to be selected for an interview.

INSTRUCTIONS: There are two copies of the application in the book. One is labeled WORK SHEET. The other is labeled MASTER COPY. Place your answers neatly on the master copy after you have "practiced" on the work sheet. This *perfectly* filled out master copy can be used as a guide for preparing a prospective employer's application form. The first application for you to read is the work sheet. Look it over and familiarize yourself with all the questions on it. Then, using a *pencil*, follow the numbered steps as they are explained and record the answers in the proper places. If you make a mistake, erase it and redo it correctly. When you are through, read the application form completely and transfer your answers neatly onto the master copy.

GETTING HELP: If you have reading and writing problems, ask a family member or friend to help you follow the steps and write down the correct answers on the work sheet. If necessary, have someone help you fill out each application form when you begin your job search. It is unlikely that, having these problems, you will look for a job where a lot of reading and writing or math are required. The application is the only time you will be asked to write anything for this job. If you do not get help or consider this preparation too hard, you run the risk of being screened out, even if writing is not required on the job. Personnel people miss out on a lot of willing and good workers because of poor preparation of the application. Don't let them miss out on you!

Important: Applications contain instructions for completing them. The instructions may be as simple as the word "Print." But there may be more detailed instructions. Follow them to the letter. The "harmless" instruction can be a screening tool. The screener may figure that if you cannot or do not follow instructions on an application, then you can't or won't follow instructions on the job and that you are not a thorough person. It is acceptable to type if the instruction states: "Print or Type." If it says only "Print," they are interested in seeing your handwriting. If your printing is poor, have a friend complete individual applications for you.

1. VITAL INFORMATION, HIDDEN MEANINGS AND ILLEGAL QUESTIONS:
How to Avoid Embarrassment

(1) Date

Put the date you complete the application here. Use numbers for dates. Don't write out the month because of limited space to do so on some applications. Do it in one of the following examples: 2/2/82 (use of slashes) or 2-2-82 (use of hyphens). Be consistent with the style you choose with all other dates on your application.

(2) Type of work desired

If you know the title of the job opening, use that to identify you as an applicant for that particular job. If you are applying cold, without knowing if there is an opening, be simple and direct with the general name of your skills. They will relate your description of your skills with the title they used in the company once they have seen your background. NEVER write "open." It is vague and too dependent.

(3) Social Security number

Self-explanatory. If you do not have a Social Security number, get one before you look for work. If you need a "green card" to identify you as an eligible working alien, get one before you look for work and use that number as well.

(4) Name

Check each application for the way they want your name. Some ask for a full middle name, others ask for only the middle initial. Follow instructions exactly as requested.

(5) Birthdate

Do not leave it out if it is on the application! We ran across more people, particularly over the age of 35, who feared they would be considered too old by screeners. We say to all of you over-thirty-fivers that your fears are exaggerated. Twenty years ago, maybe, you would have had a hard time, but not now. Ever since firms started hiring superyoung "energetic" people, they have found the young could not cope with job stress as well as older adults. Productivity lagged, and now employers are realizing that the older, more experienced worker can handle personal problems that can interfere with work loads better than very young workers.

There are positive reasons for filling in your birthdate. If you leave it off the application, employers will immediately start checking other information and come up with a pretty accurate figure on their own. If you leave it blank, the screener might think that (a) it could mean you have problems about identifying and accepting your age; (b) you are sloppy and not following instructions; and (c) you are making a personal statement of protest about being asked your age.

(6) Height

Use the signs for feet and inches—for example: 5′ 9″, 6′ 0″, etc. If you leave either out, you will be judged as lacking a sense of detail. If you write just the 5 and the 9, it makes you seem 59 *inches* tall.

(7) Weight

You should know that you will be expected to state your weight on your application. If you are exceptionally over-

(WORK SHEET)

APPLICATION FOR EMPLOYMENT

(1) Date ______________

VITAL INFORMATION, HIDDEN MEANINGS AND ILLEGAL QUESTIONS

Print only, use pencil.

(2) Type of work desired ______________ (3) Social Security no. ______________

(4) Name ____

LAST FIRST MIDDLE (MAIDEN NAME IF MARRIED)

(5) Birthdate ________ (6) Height ________ (7) Weight ________ (8) Phone ________

(9) Present address ______________ City ______________ Zip Code ________

(10) How long have you lived at the above address? ______________

(11) Previous address ______________

(12) Salary required: $ _____ per _____ (13) When available to begin work? ______________

(14) Husband's or wife's name ______________ (15) Occupation ______________

(16) Number of children ________ Ages ______________

(17) Are you bondable? ______________

(18) General health: Poor ________ Fair ________ Good ________ Excellent ________

(19) Do you have any physical or health limitations? ________ If yes, describe ______________

____

(20) Have you or any of your family been treated for an emotional or mental problem? ________
If yes, explain ______________

(21) Have you ever received worker's compensation? ______________

(22) How many days of work or school have you missed in the past year? ______________

(23) Military status ______________ If veteran, when inducted ______________
Branch ________ Date discharged ________ Type of discharge ________

(24) Have you been convicted of a crime on or after your 18th birthday? ______________
If yes, give date, nature and disposition ______________

____

(25) Languages spoken ______________ (26) Special talents ______________

(27) Do you plan any future schooling? ______________

(28) Interest in other work ______________

(29) Do you type? ________ (30) Take dictation? ________ (31)Operate office machines? ________
Specify ______________

(32) What are your interests or hobbies? ______________

(33) What clubs or organizations are you a member of? ______________

EDUCATION

(34) TYPE OF SCHOOL	(35) NAME OF SCHOOL	(36) LOCATION	(37) YEARS ATTENDED FROM MO./YR.	TO MO./YR.	(38) GRADUATE YES	NO	(39) DEGREE	(40) MAJOR OR COURSES	(41) GRADE POINT AVERAGE
HIGH SCHOOL					☐	☐			
COLLEGE					☐	☐			
GRADUATE SCHOOL					☐	☐			
BUSINESS OR TRADE SCHOOL					☐	☐			
MILITARY SCHOOLS					☐	☐			
OTHER					☐	☐			

REFERENCES

(42)

PLEASE LIST TWO PERSONAL REFERENCES WHOM WE MAY CONTACT—EXCLUDE RELATIVES

NAME ADDRESS TELEPHONE NUMBER YEARS KNOWN

NAME ADDRESS TELEPHONE NUMBER YEARS KNOWN

weight, you might plan to lose some weight before you go job hunting—not only because you are interested in your appearance, but because some employers reason that overweight can generate health and performance problems and they will be reluctant to give you an interview. If your new weight is a bit closer to the norm, and your application shows it, it will be that much easier for you to get an interview, where you can convince the employer of your ability, regardless of weight. You are in luck, of course, if the interviewer is very overweight because then your weight usually will not matter. But don't depend on it! Use the sign for pounds, or the abbreviation *lbs.*

(8) Phone

Before every telephone number listed on an application, use the Area Code like this: (415), then your *phone* number. Even if you have only one area code in your area, put it in anyway. Doing so shows a capacity for detail.

Employers will call you during their working hours. Though you are not employed, it is not necessary that you sit by your telephone after you apply for a job. It is boring and creates too much tension waiting for it to ring. Besides, you will be out on interviews or whatever else you do when not working. Therefore, you should have a "message" phone if yours is unattended. This can be the phone of a relative or a helpful friend. You must not miss employer calls for interviews.

Create a line in this space that allows you to write in a message phone. This will show that you are careful about detail and are providing a convenience for both you and the prospective employer. Nothing is more frustrating to an individual trying to hire an applicant than to call a candidate for a job and not be able to contact the person. You run the risk of being selected but not contacted if you do not provide a phone number to call when you're not at home. Here is how it should look for this space:

Phone: Home—[415] 222-2222
Message—[415] 333-3333

If you are employed and are seeking to change jobs, give your work phone and identify it as such so a prospective employer will be discreet when calling you.

Phone: Home—(415) 222-2222
Work—(415) 444-4444

Providing a potential employer with a phone contact during working hours is considered so important that in our workshop setting, a special incoming telephone line is reserved specifically for that purpose. The participants used the same "message" number and acted as message takers for each other.

(9) Present address, city, Zip Code

Do not forget apartment numbers or the Zip Code. Details—but, as always, important.

(10) How long have you lived at the above address?

Why do they ask that? Right. To get an idea of your stability. Or, they could use that information to see if your answer corresponds with your work history. Some people put down a lengthy time at an address to seem stable and then, writing out their work history, indicate that they worked hundreds of miles from where they said they lived. Be accurate. It does not matter if you lived at your present address for a long time. Just make sure it matches your work history.

(11) Previous address

Be prepared to give your previous address. A screener is not going to track down a former landlord or ask to see proof.

The prospective employer just wants to see if *you* know it and how much control you have over the details of your life. Be sure to include city, state *and* Zip Code.

(12) Salary required (your first lesson on how to go after an offer—not a job)

This is another screening tool!

When you know what the exact pay or pay range is for the job (from job-opening announcements, newspaper advertisements, etc.), place that exact figure or entire range in this space. *Example:* $5.25 per hour (advertised); $800–$1,000 (range).

When there is absolutely no indication what the job pays, place the abbreviation for "negotiable" in the space given: "Negot."

Do not place a price on your head. There are too many unknown factors about the job at this stage. You could be too high or too low. Either could screen you out. You run the risk of down-playing your abilities or asking for more than they are willing to pay. Keep your options *open.*

Professionally, on their part and yours, salary should be discussed at the time of an *offer.* That is when they call and want *you.* Once you are selected and you have an interview, the interviewer will either tell you, up front, what the job pay range is or will play the screening game and ask you your requirements. You have already indicated on the application that salary is negotiable. They will now screen you to see if their job meets your income need. Why should they hire you and train you if you will leave as soon as you find a better-paying job? You have no way to know what they are paying, and your task is to find out, if possible, during the interview and to keep from pricing yourself out. Here is a typical exchange of how you find out, the actual salary or the range, and what they do to get you to state your requirements.

Setting: You are being interviewed. Everything is going great! You like them, they like you. Suddenly, out of nowhere, comes, "What is your salary requirement?" Instant stress! Caught unaware. Sweat. Imaginary itches. Body language goes to hell. Shift in chair. Too long a pause.

YOU: "Negotiable." (So far, so good. It's on your application.)

INTERVIEWER: O.K., let's negotiate. (Game is back to you.)

YOU: What is your salary range? (Game is back to them.)

A professional will stop at this point, tell you the salary range and wait for a reaction. The best thing to do is to answer immediately, "That is within my range." Later, if they offer you the job, you can negotiate higher in the range. If they tell you the range, the game ends here.

But most interviewers either consider your questions about salary range as a challenge, or they consider it vital to their screening to know. Then they may reply something like this:

INTERVIEWER: We do not have a salary range. Therefore, what is your salary requirement? (Game is back to *you* again.)

There is only one way to end this:

YOU: Why don't we discuss salary at the time of an offer?

This is where salary should be discussed, and all interviewers know it. Or should. If they push, lose their cool and demand to know, get up, shake hands, wish them all the luck in the world filling their position and *walk out.* You have performed as a professional. Keep your dignity and do not give in to this game. If you place a price on your head—up front—you have very little negotiating leverage when they make the offer. Have a say in the pay you will receive. Go after the *offer.* Then, if you cannot live on what they offer, turn down the job. To keep from losing a good job, however, ask how soon after starting you would be reviewed for an increase, and the amount of the increase. If it is automatic, on merit or a combination of both, this will help you make up your mind. Then say you will call back within a day after considering the offer. If the interviewer persists, you could, instead of walking out, look him or her in the eye and say, "Are you making me an offer?" Good luck on that one. If you use it, try not to snarl.

Many people, just to appear humble, state an amount. Some employers are ruthless enough to hire you at that amount, and then give you a raise in three to six months *up to what you could have been making at the start.* You feel good and they feel *better* for saving the company money. Try it our way and you'll be in charge and get what you're worth.

(13) When available to begin work

If unemployed, put "Immed.," for immediately. Do not put "ASAP." Too panicky. Writing "Now" means you are available to go to work on the spot. "Immed." is a softer word. Besides, you are going for multiple offers.

If you are employed and applying to change jobs, place a minimum of one week notice in the space: "1 wk. notice." If you indicate that you will leave your current job without notice, you will not get the offer. It is professional to give notice, and not giving adequate notice is a chief reason for a bad or qualified reference. Some people simply walk out, leaving the previous employer stranded. The new employer will reason that if you are willing to leave your current job without notice to take theirs, you might do the same to *them* someday.

(14) Husband or wife's name

If you are single, place a small dash here. *Don't leave it blank.* If you are married, write your husband's or wife's first name in. If you are divorced, place a small dash. Do *not* write: "Divorced," "Separated," "Dead," etc. It is none of their business and can set up preconceived notions about you and lead to an awkward discussion at an interview.

If you are separated, we suggest that you write the name in anyway. After all, that person is still your husband or wife. *Never* deal with any unpleasant marital situation when job-seeking. This has nothing whatever to do with selling yourself and your skills. If you are being interviewed and something triggers an opportunity for you to "sing your woes," you could be judged "currently emotionally risky" and be screened out because of a simple lament about your negative married life.

(15) Occupation

As presented here, this means the occupation of your husband or wife—not your occupation. Stay away from overinflating your spouse's occupation with a specific title. Many people do this to impress. Employers like to hire people who *need* jobs, thinking that such a person will make a better worker. If you inflate your spouse's title, you run the risk of explaining why you want or need the job. For example: "certified public accountant" can become "accounting," which could mean any job level in accounting; "machinist supervisor" can become "machine worker."

(16) Number of children; ages

State the number of children you have and their ages. Example: 3 children/6, 10, 13. Some firms try to determine whether you are married by asking about children. If yours is a single-parent family, their main concern would be that you may miss a good deal of work because of children's illness, school problems, etc. Don't worry about this. It will not screen you out. What *will* screen you out is a statement such as this during an interview: "Yes, my children are lovely and I intend to arrange for a baby-sitter/day-care center *when* I get a job." You must indicate that they are provided for so you can work NOW—not when you *get* the job.

(17) Are you bondable? (Ex-offenders, take note!)

Many people do not know what this means. It refers to the employer's ability to get a bonding company to insure them against possible dishonesty on your part. If you have a previous conviction, it could mean that the bonding company used by the firm would not guarantee any loss the firm had because of you. However, you can mark it yes, conviction or no conviction, because you yourself can obtain bonding through another source—the government. Call your local Employment Development Department (a lot of people call it the *un*employment office, because the only time you go there is when you are unemployed). They will give you information on how you can obtain bonding through the government.

In effect, bonding means you may have to handle cash or negotiable securities and/or have a security clearance for the job. You fill out a bonding application, and the bonding company checks your past. (Make no mistake about it—they *will* check.) If you do not have a previous conviction, if they hire you and if you *do* steal from the company, the bonding company pays the business their loss, and the bonding company comes after you.

If, during a later interview, the company tells you that bonding is required for the job, tell them you will furnish your own bond. If you mark "yes" in this space and *also* write "yes" on application item 24 (conviction record), they will wonder how you can be bonded, but you can answer that question during the interview. For those with conviction records, later in the book we will tell you how to obtain an interview *before* you fill out an application and how to deal with your past *in person* instead of on paper. When we get to item 24, we will discuss the matter further, but consider this now: Why should they select you at the unseen stage when so many do *not* indicate an arrest record? They are your *competition,* and that's why we must tell you how to get an interview without first completing an application.

(18) General health:
Poor __ Fair __ Good __ Excellent __

The correct answer here is "Excellent." If your general health were not excellent, you would not be looking for a job. In our workshop setting of 12 to 16 people each week, at least four or five people would mark the line "Good" instead of "Excellent." When we asked them why, it usually turned out that they "didn't feel good" *that* day. They had a cold . . . were getting over the flu . . . had a headache—a total misinterpretation of the question. Look at it this way: The question means, "Can you work 40 hours a week?" Some did not want to "brag" about their health and figured it would make them appear humble. GETTING A JOB IS NO TIME TO BE HUMBLE. (We will discuss this later, too, in the interview portion of the book.) The correct answer is "Excellent"; otherwise, don't bother to look for work.

(19) Do you have any physical or health limitations? If so, describe.

Obviously, if you are minus a leg or an arm, in a wheelchair, on canes or possess other obvious physical problems, you can see no way of getting around saying so. Right? WRONG. Again, if you cannot do the job you would not be applying, and what's more, you have compensated for your limitations. The key word here is "limitations." If you can do the job and can work 40 hours per week, then what are your limitations? Arm or no arm, the answer is "No," and place a dash next to "If yes, describe." The question often appears with the words "that would prevent you from doing the job" after the word "limitations."

Your goal is to get the interview, where you can sell your skills. If they ask the question again, when you see them, tell them simply that you have no limitations. *Don't "carry on" about any aspect of your problem—how it happened, etc.* It is human nature to talk about physical problems, and the more you do, the more they will see you as obsessed about them. Then the interview will be bogged down in negatives instead of positives. Stick to the reason you are there: your ability to fill the job opening. If you don't, you might get sympathy, but you won't get the job.

For those who are still not convinced, put a "No" in this space. Ask yourself this question: Can I perform the jobs I go for as well as my competition? If the answer is yes, carry on. If the answer is no, then you should look for a job where you are *not* limited. In the interview, deal with what you *can* do. Do not allow the conversation to dwell on any aspect of limitation!

(20) Have you or any of your family been treated for an emotional or mental problem? If yes, explain.

It is infuriating that this question is still asked in one form or another. But it is. If we had not seen it or a similar version on applications, we would not bother to place it on our sample form. What is unbelievable is that people actually volunteer information in detail. "Yes, my grandfather was an ax-murderer"; "Yes, my aunt went berserk at the grocery store"; "Yes, my father beat my mother... two broken arms, bruises and damaged kidneys"! First, the answer is *always* "No." *It is none of their business.* After answering "No," place a dash after "Explain": a detail. (This is one of the questions on an application you should definitely call to the attention of the Labor Department.) Sometimes a separate questionnaire may be required for jobs where physical or other health information is needed and may be asked legally. If you cannot meet the physical or other health requirements for such jobs, do not waste your time applying.

(21) Have you ever received worker's compensation?

The question is on some applications—and is more troublesome to people who have received workers' compensation than is generally realized.

Workers' compensation refers to time missed and money paid to an employee because of a work-related injury. Employers must pay insurance premiums on all employees to a state agency to cover work-related injuries. Then, if an employee is injured on the job, he or she receives medical care and cash benefits during recovery. It all ends up costing the employer money and lost production time.

Unfortunately, some employers hesitate to hire people with a past history of collecting on a work-related injury claim because they fear that the applicant might have a recurrence of the old injury or a new injury on the job. Inquiries we conducted at both large and small firms in Northern California revealed that although they do not do a routine check of records of workers' compensation, they may require the applicant to have a physical examination, at which time previous injuries that have left scars or physical conditions that limit the kind of work a person can do will come to light. Blood tests and other biological tests may also be required. To my knowledge, these practices are typical of other areas of the country as well.

If the injury does recur and the employee has not been entirely truthful on his of her application, another problem presents itself: the applicant risks being denied benefits for the new injury. And there could be grounds for dismissal as well.

The best course of action, it would appear, is to try to get an interview before you will fill out an application (see "The Telephone Method for Tapping the Hidden Job Market" on page 159-163)—so that you have an opportunity to explain about your former injury and to demonstrate that you are in the best of health. Instructions in this method are given later in the book.

(22) How many days of work or school have you missed in the past year?

They want to know *your* version of missed work. They will try to match your answer with that of a former employer (if they can get it) during the reference check. Companies know that a common reason for terminating people is excessive missed time at work, even if for reasons beyond the employee's control. This is known as *down time* in business and industry; your work is not getting done, or someone else is doubling up to get it done. Even if your work record was good, missed time might cause a "qualified" reference by your previous employer to a prospective new employer.

Let us demonstrate: When a reference checker or screener telephones your former employer where missed time was a factor in your performance, they might hear this: "Oh, so-and-so was a *lovely* person... so nice... he/she did beautiful work... everyone liked her/him." Then the reference checker may ask: "How was his/her attendance? Was much work missed?" The answer could be anywhere from "We cannot give out that information" to "Well, that was the *problem.*" Such a statement could screen you out or set up serious roadblocks when a decision has to be made to hire you or your nearest competitor.

After Part Three of the application, we will tell you how to call your previous employers and find out where you stand regarding a reference. IT IS CRITICAL FOR YOU TO KNOW THIS TO AVOID CONSTANT WASTE OF TIME IN APPLYING FOR JOBS AND, ULTIMATELY, REJECTION. There are many ways to eliminate your past mistakes, and you are going to have to do what is necessary to do so. We will call this to your attention again: Why should you file an application, have an interview and have expectations of an offer, only to be rejected? What a waste of time. And so demoralizing!

By finding out what information, if any, is given out for each job you had, even if the truth hurts, you may have to eliminate that job altogether from your work history! We will show you how to do all this.

For now, if you had good attendance and do not remember how many days you missed three jobs ago, put down no more than eight days. Do not include vacation days; you were entitled to those. Remember, you are not present when the application is read; you can't explain *anything* at that stage.

(23) Military status

If you were in the military, give the information asked for on each line here as needed. If your discharge was dishonorable and you state otherwise, a security clearance (required for some jobs) will reveal that you were not truthful. The best rule where a dishonorable or any other negative-class discharge is the problem is: Don't look for a job that requires a security clearance!

(24) Have you been convicted of a crime on or after your 18th birthday? If yes, give date, nature and disposition.

This is asked in a number of different ways. Again, we must consider various situations to cover the subject. If you are 18 or over and had a conviction before 18, the answer is "No" and is the truth.

OVER 18 YEARS OF AGE: If you were convicted, you may have a problem if you apply to a government agency—city, county, state or federal—or a business where a security clearance is required, even though you have not spent any time in jail. Government agencies will check routinely, either before or after you are hired, and a company that requires a security clearance will have you complete a form and will check your background. Therefore, we recommend that you not waste your time applying to a business or industry where a security clearance is required. They have too many people applying who have your skills and who also can pass a security clearance. Government agencies are more liberal and are less likely to discriminate. Just be prepared to discuss your total rehabilitation and desire to do the right thing *now*—in spite of your past mistakes.

(More on this later under "How to Deal with Gaps in Employment.") You should know that other than the cases we have just discussed, any other employer *will not know* about your conviction because of the Right to Privacy Act, which forbids such routine investigations. If you did not serve time in jail or prison, it is unlikely that you have too serious an employment gap, if any, to explain, other than in the method discussed on pages 64–65.

IF YOU WERE CONVICTED AND *CURRENTLY* ARE ON PROBATION OR PAROLE: Your best bet, under the circumstances, is to utilize the method we outline in "The Telephone Method for Tapping The Hidden Job Market," pages 159–163, in Section Two. By doing this, you will avoid having to state the facts before you have a chance to sell yourself and your skills. In other words, the interview will come before the application or at the same time. Otherwise, applying unseen, you can be screened out and will never know exactly why. You will become frustrated and discouraged because you can't get through the front doorway. It is unlikely that you will be given a chance to prove your sincere intentions to start over clean. Later, under "How to Handle Gaps Between Jobs,"—pages 64–65, we will tell you the way to present your past problems. Right now concentrate on presenting yourself professionally.

FOR PEOPLE CURRENTLY ON PROBATION OR PAROLE

Some parole or probation officers are sympathetic. They understand that you will have a problem getting back into productive society and will do anything they can do to help you. The main thing they insist on is that you get a job, but many take the position, and justifiably so, that if you do not tell the truth to an employer about your past, you are setting them and the system up for a liability situation. If the probation or parole officer says you do not have to tell a prospective employer that you are on probation, then write "No" on the line. If yours tells you that you *must* tell, then write "Yes, will discuss in the interview" on this line. We will tell you how to handle this during the interview section in the book. It is the only method we will endorse in this regard.

If you give the exact charge for which you served time in jail or prison, it does not matter what your skill—you will be screened out at the application stage. Why should a business or industry pick you when so many have said "No"? If you list the nature of your crime—murder I or II, rape, armed robbery, embezzlement, sale of drugs, petty theft, welfare fraud, assault, etc.—the screener will eliminate your application. Some Good Samaritan employers welcome ex-offenders, but not enough to increase your overall odds of being hired over a nonoffender. But if you effectively indicate to them by your application, your resume and your attitude that you should be considered, your chances of being interviewed are greater.

A WORD TO PAROLE OR PROBATION OFFICERS

We have handled many direct referrals to our program of those in work furlough programs or on parole or probation. We conducted an informal poll among these clients. Our question to them was: "To your knowledge, what percentage of your fellow inmates would go straight if they had the means to get a job and not get turned down?" Their answers said that 60 percent would. Sixty percent of former convicts back in productive society would make quite an impact on the crime rate in the United States. All you can do is counsel and monitor movement, and some of you go out of your way to help in other ways. Some of you are hard-nosed with your clients. Consider this: If you constantly monitor a client, *if* they do get work, by calling their boss and making sure they are working, what kind of a chance do you think your client has to get ahead in that firm? He or she is already considered a second-class citizen by your actions and visibility to the employer. Your clients have paid the penalty and been conditionally released. The condition is that they do not commit further offenses. Your job is to see that they do not. We don't envy you your position. BUT there is a way to confirm that parolees or probationers are working without destroying their self-esteem. Here is how: Call clients *personally* at their work to check if they have the job and are still working. Do not talk to the boss or identify yourself. If they are working in a small company, the person who answers the phone may know about you. Ask your clients to tell you exactly how to reach them at their job. In larger companies, ask the telephone operator to connect you to the individual. If the operator does not know the person, ask to be connected to personnel and then ask personnel to locate their department and ask to be transferred. If your clients cannot accept calls on the job, leave a message for them to call you (leave your *name* only). If the client is not employed there and has lied to you, then you have the information you need to react to this. But if you do reach your client at work, you know he or she has a job, and the boss is spared the constant reminder that the ex-offender may or may not be trustworthy. With this procedure, your client has been given a chance to succeed. You will not be endangering the client's renewed self-esteem, *and* you are still monitoring effectively. Consider these approaches seriously in the perspective of your client's rehabilitative need.

---

(25) Languages spoken

Note that the question does *not* ask: What languages other than English do you read, speak or write? Therefore, since English is a language, English goes in *first,* then additional languages. This goes for anyone who has come from another country to work in the United States. If you place your native language first, the screener might think you are not comfortable with English and therefore will have translation problems with work instructions.

(26) Special talents

Most people leave this space blank. Don't. Answer either (a) "Job-related skills" or (b) "Ability to deal with people." We recommend (b), which indicates social interaction—an important ingredient in working in a team or departmental setting. It does not matter how skilled you are if you cannot demonstrate social interaction with co-workers. Social interaction is definitely measurable during selection. It may be touched on verbally or explored in a written pre-employment test. Therefore, this is a good answer for this space. Why should they hire someone they might suspect would create havoc with co-workers?

Also, since interviewers find "I get along well with people" to be a dreary cop-out statement, get it said this way on the application, then drop it unless the interviewer brings it up. We have viewed many video-tapes of mock interviews where the person being interviewed could think of no other answer to certain verbal screening questions than, "I get along well with people." You are *expected* to get along well with people, so that is no prize answer.

(27) Do you plan any future schooling?

If you place "Yes" in this space and nothing else, you will leave the screener wondering if you are taking the job just to get a little short-term money to go back to school, and also wondering how long you would stay if hired. It costs a company money to train you for a position, no matter how skilled you are. You must apply your skills to their systems. This takes time. During this time, you are not really as productive as the job calls for; you are learning. State it this way: "Yes, in conjunction with vocation." That means you are willing to go back to school to take courses that will make you promotable or further your skills for *that* job. Many employers are willing to pay for tuition, providing you pass the courses. It is in their interest to help you with costs. Ask about further education related to the job at the interview.

If you are planning to go back to school full-time and need to work and save money to do so, say "Yes," but let them know it is far enough in the future that they will get their money's worth out of your employment. Remember, because it costs a company money to hire people, they want to be sure you are going to stay awhile. You can come back to that company once you complete school *if* you are studying something you can use in the company once you have obtained the education.

If you simply say "No" to this question, it may make a negative statement about your personal progress and reduces your options.

(28) Interest in other work

The most frequent answer our clients give is "No." Just plain "No"—a total misinterpretation of the question from the employer's viewpoint. Others placed "fantasy" answers in this space, answers totally unrelated to their skills for the job in question. One example was: "Want to open a gift shop within one year." Others put down "Yes," period. "Yes" what? "No" can mean zero forward momentum or ambition. This tells the screeners you do not know what you want (a job, not an offer), or you are sloppy in your thinking. If you know of a related promotable job in the firm to which you are applying, then place that job title in this space.

Many people do not really know what they want. If you are one of them, place either one of the following in this space: "Growth potential" or "Advancement opportunity." This will offset what you do *not* know about the company, indicates forward momentum and can indicate you will work hard for promotion. Since it is easier to promote people from within, because you know the systems, products or services, these statements are positive. It will cost the company much less to rehire for your old position and to promote you. These two recommendations for answers are yet other examples of go *for the offer, not the job.*

(29) Do you type?

If you type *under* 30 words per minute, write the word "Light" in this space. Do not attempt to "pad" your typing. You may have to take a test.

If you type over 30 words per minute, answer "Yes" and give the number of words per minute like this: "Yes (31 wpm)." They did not ask your speed; you are *giving information freely!* Some applications have a space for your speed, but, if they do not, tell them.

Many women in our classes left this blank rather than say on an application that they could type. Their explanation was that, while they could type, they did not want an employer to know this because they felt they would be taken advantage of if they were seeking work other than that requiring typing. They have a point. For some reason, employers find it easy to ask a women who types to do so, even if hired in another position. Sometimes work backs up, or vacations and illness reduce the typing staff. However, we agree with you. Write in this space "*Own work.*" That way, you call attention to your skill but make it loud and clear what and when you type.

(30) Take Dictation?

If you do, give the number of *strokes per minute.* If you use a dictaphone and do not take dictation, write the word *dictaphone.* If you do *both* say so. If you do not do either, write the word *no.*

(31) Operate office machines? Specify

Two- or three-hole punches and staplers are not considered office machines. Write in by *name* the ones you operate. If you cannot operate any other machine, you certainly can operate a copy machine, or learn how to do it in a few minutes. Write "Copy machine" on your application. Then, if you are hired and are asked to run the copier, don't worry. All you have to do is approach the machine, put the paper in, set the number of copies on the dial, push the button marked, "Print" and off it goes. If it doesn't, just ask for help, and some co-worker will surely show you what you did wrong. If they usher you into a room where a gigantic machine is whirring away, lights flashing and buzzing, waiting to be fed—don't panic. Say, "My, this is a *big* machine. I'm used to a much smaller one." You will then receive instruction.

(32) What are your interests or hobbies?

How people rack their brains to put down as much as they can think of to make themselves seem an "all around" person! "Boating, biking, fishing, hunting, sports of all kinds, reading, music," etc. WRONG! A screener is liable to assume that you are so active outside of work that you will perform work half heartedly, just to get back to your outside activities, or that you will be so exhausted from all the action that you won't show up on Mondays, or if you do, that you'll be too tired to perform your work properly. Don't list over two. It's O.K. to put in a dash or "None" if you have no interests or hobbies. You cannot go wrong if they are work-related. Do not choose weird or bizarre hobbies or interests.

(33) What clubs or organizations are you a member of?

The answer "None" is all right. You don't have to be a joiner. Just don't list any you belong to that are considered radical or race identifying. Why? Because discrimination is unfortunately still alive and well out there. Remember that during the selection process they do not have to tell you *why* you were rejected.

Remember that you will never see *all* of the 33 items on one application. You may see a lot of them and you may see very few, since many are of questionable legality. If you do not find them on the application, you may be asked them during an interview. The same answers apply. Keep in mind the answers you wrote on this master application. You will use it as a guide so that you are also ready in an interview if their questions are similar to those on our application form. During the interview portion of this book, we will deal with stock questions (and a few others) that are asked in an interview.

This completes Part 1 of the application. We are now ready for Part 2, on education.

2. QUESTIONS ON EDUCATION: DO'S AND DON'TS

a. How to fill out this section

Some applications ask you merely to circle the highest grade completed. Some applications give you the space and opportunity to elaborate on each school you have attended. They allow for listings of all types of education to screen for all skills that may be related in any way to a job they have available. Many companies have hundreds of job titles within their company, and giving room for many types of schools allows them to use one application form.

As you read through the instructions and information in the section on education, accept the idea that you are going for an entry-level or semiskilled job that you can do or learn to do. Be complete in this section no matter what your education level. We are not going to put you down for not having enough education, or lecture you on returning to school. We are interested only in your obtaining work until *you* decide what path you should take.

Before you complete any part of the education section, find the category that fits you and then use the work sheet in the proper manner. You will find that most applications have a simpler education section than the one presented here. But this form will give you the opportunity to record all information on education in the event you apply to a firm using a more complete application.

b. If you hold a high school diploma or G.E.D. (General Equivalency Diploma)

Very little or no work experience: You are qualified to learn a semiskilled job. This means you will have to *sell* your desire to use both your education and limited work experience to an employer offering a position that trains at entry level. By "selling" we mean that you must demonstrate your talent for detail in your presentation to get you through the doorway. Then, using our presentation methods, you must demonstrate to the employer in the interview that you understand you will be in a learning setting and that you hope to be promoted as you learn the company's products and systems. You need not say more than this. It is what they want to hear, and no more is expected of you for this type of training position. That statement and the presentation methods we give in this book will make you a top competitor for the position. Then they will check your references and decide who to hire based on a combination of written presentations, interviews, and references. Therefore, it is important to follow our instruction about contacting former employers *before* you seek work, so there will be no major unexpected roadblock to screen you out.

If, just because you think they pay more, you apply for positions that are beyond your ability and skill level, you are wasting your time. You may think you can do the job, but applicants who are your competition will apply, perhaps not with more education but with more experience, and you won't have a chance. You will never hear from the employer past the application stage and, because you were unrealistic, your own self-esteem will be damaged.

The most difficult part of assisting our participants with a high school education and limited work experience or *no* high school education and limited work experience is getting them to think realistically. Many would spot an advertised position that offered a high income and seemed "glamorous." They wanted to apply immediately, without consideration for the qualifications the job required in education and experience. It sounded like a "nifty" job to them and something they would "like" to do. If you find such a job, use our methods in Section Two to get yourself through the doorway to find out for yourself. There are always exceptions! The information we give you in Section Two regarding want ads will help you identify those jobs for which you are qualified and those for which you need not waste your time—or the employer's.

In our weekly new-class workshop setting, participants were asked the first day their first two work objectives. Jobs considered "glamorous" were always the choice. The most common job [it was brought up every week] was one with an airline. We asked why. The reply was always: "Because I like to deal with people and love to travel."

Not one word was said about the service they had to give to customers to uphold standards in the very competitive airline business to ensure repeat business. If the interview could be obtained, that lack of a thoughtful answer would be what the airline interviewer would remember, no matter what else was said. A high school education *could* land you a job with an airline if you are realistic about the needs of the company. Just approach one of them and demonstrate how your ability to provide service and attention to detail would make a valuable contribution to repeat business and increased revenue. That's what the interviewer wants to hear; it shows you know what the airline's problem is and also shows that you feel you can make a contribution to solving it.

If you hold a high school diploma and want work where you have authority, make decisions and have job satisfaction, but deep down you know such a job will be hard, if not impossible, to get: (1) take a job as a survival measure while you obtain the education you need to compete for those better jobs, or (2) take a job with a company you know is growing, either because you discovered this through research or because the company told you so. Either way, your chances of obtaining what you want or achieving faster growth are greater than being unrealistic and demoralized because you are impatient. If you take the second option and, within a year, there does not appear to be growth, *change jobs.* Section Three in this book will tell you how.

Probably the one exception to what we have just stated is in "blue-collar" jobs because of the higher visibility of hard work and quickly identifiable leadership qualities. Blue-collar jobs offer less formal and inhibiting settings as well as fewer "political" problems. Because blue-collar jobs are likely to have more routine work and are based on immediate completion of projects, your job performance is more easily judged. The smart blue-collar worker who makes the most of an often very informal interview does not just sit and mumble answers; such a person indicates that he or she enjoys manual work or would enjoy being *trained* to do it and likes to work hard. Employment opportunities in this area are much brighter if this approach is used.

You can qualify for some jobs with only a high school education (some require apprenticeships; some do not). Here are some of the job titles:

machinist [all-around]	blue-collar-worker supervisor	office machine operator
machine tool operator	photographic laboratory occupations	postal clerk
lithographer	power truck operator	receptionist

photoengraver	bookkeeping worker	secretary
printing press operator	cashier	shipping/receiving worker
bookbinder	collection worker	statistical clerk
assembler	file clerk	stock clerk
auto painter	hotel front-office clerk	
typist (50–60 wpm)	fire fighter	auto salesperson
bank clerk	guard	auto service adviser
bank teller	police officer	route driver
insurance claim representative	state police officer	travel agent
hotel housekeeping assistant	construction inspector	air traffic controller
pest controller	mail carrier	airplane mechanic
cook and chef	telephone operator	airplane pilot
correction officer	library technician/assist.	flight attendant

These samplings by no means make up the complete list. For a more complete listing, along with more information on each job, ask your local Department of Labor office for a free publication titled *Jobs for Which You Can Qualify if You Are a High School Graduate.* It contains good information.

c. If You *Did Not* Graduate from High School or Do *Not* Have a G.E.D.

Place a small dash in spaces 34, 35, 36, 37, 38, 39, 40, and 41 for "High School" and complete each space in the education section for any schooling you may have received *other* than high school. *List all courses* to show you sought schooling even if you did not graduate from high school. If you have *partially* completed high school, indicate where and when. Give complete information for each school, including Zip Code in space 36, "Location."

Not graduating from high school will not keep you from getting a job if you are realistic about the jobs you seek. It is not necessary to have graduated from high school to get a decent-paying job, or at least one that will get you started in a vocation where you can advance as you learn or return to school for a diploma or G.E.D. to improve yourself. We know many smart people who did not graduate but who are doing well in business because they were patient. They learned on the job and took courses in their spare time to improve their job performance. They did not take generalized courses or courses that bored them.

If you are tempted to falsely claim a high school education—don't! If you have not actually completed high school, it will be readily apparent from you work that you do not have the reading, writing and math skills of a high school graduate. It would be better to try at first for a job that does not require a high school education and then go about completing your education.

The Department of Labor also prints a booklet titled *Jobs That Usually Do Not Require a High School Education.* Ask for it. Each job listed gives specific information about that job, and will be a big help to you. Here are some of the job titles:

molder
machine tool operator
assembler
auto painter
boilermaker
movie projectionist
photo lab worker
painter
welder
file clerk
postal clerk
shipping/receiving clerk
stock clerk
bank teller
custodian
hotel housekeeper
pest controller
bartender
cook/chef
dining-room helper
food counter worker

meat cutter	waiter/waitress	barber
bellhop	cosmetologist	household helper
guard	mail carrier	gasoline service attendant
model (good luck)	retail store clerk	route driver
bricklayer, stonemason	carpenter	construction laborer
drywall installer	floor covering installer	insulation worker (be careful)
ironworker	construction machinist	paperhanger
roofer	tilesetter	merchant marine sailor
bus driver	truck driver	parking attendant
taxi driver	telephone line installer	PBX operator
auto body repairer	auto mechanic	shoe repairer
nurse's aide	orderly/attendant	social service aide
floral design assistant	all performing artists	furniture mover

For details about these jobs plus information on trades requiring high school diplomas, some college or specialized training, college degrees and apprenticeships, ask your nearest Department of Labor office to send you the appropriate pamphlets. They're well written and give valuable information.

(42) References

The application asks you to list two personal references. The key here is *detail.* Provide complete addresses, Zip Codes, and area codes for telephone numbers. They probably won't contact these references unless the job requires a security clearance. After all, would you list anyone who would say anything *bad* about you? They are interested only if you *know* two people who will say something *good* about you. If you leave it blank, then they will very likely assume you do not know two people who would say something good about you. Do not put in the names of relatives.

3. WORK HISTORY SECTION: DEALING WITH PROBLEM QUESTIONS

If they've read this far, you're O.K. What you list here, coupled with your resume, is the 'meat' of the application. It can make or break you at the unseen stage or even *after* you have an interview.

Follow instructions carefully for completing this section in each application you fill out. The way you do it can be used as a screening tool because the person reading your application might feel that if you can't follow instructions on an application, you won't follow instructions on a job. Again, remember that details count in making a good impression on the reader of the application.

List the *last* job first, then list your previous jobs, using the following instructions for the numbered boxes:

(43) Present or Last Employer

Full name of company or individual. Do not use initials.

(44) Address

Full street address, town, state. Use the correct Zip Code.

(45) Kind of Business

Self-explanatory. We assume you know the kind of business in which you worked.

(46) Starting Date/Leaving Date
Month and year for both.

This is important and, in many cases, the *only* information a former employee will reveal. Some people, because they cannot remember, leave this blank! It's the worst thing you

PRESENT or LAST EMPLOYMENT

PREVIOUS EMPLOYMENT RECORD

List former places of employment including temporary and permanent positions. Leave no lapse of time unaccounted for. Begin with present or most recent position.

Present or last employer (43)	Address (44)	Kind of business (45)

Starting date Month / Year	Leaving date Month / Year (46)	Starting pay (47)	Final pay (48)	Reason for leaving (49)	May we contact? (50)

Present or last job title (51)	Immediate supervisor (52)	Supervisor's title (53)

Description of work and responsibilities (54)

Which duties did you like most? (55)

Which duties did you like least? (56)

PREVIOUS EMPLOYMENT

Next previous employer	Address	Kind of business

Starting date Month / Year	Leaving date Month / Year	Starting pay	Final pay	Reason for leaving

Last job title	Immediate supervisor	Title

Description of work and responsibilities

Which duties did you like most?

Which duties did you like least?

Next previous employer	Address	Kind of business

Starting date Month / Year	Leaving date Month / Year	Starting pay	Final pay	Reason for leaving

Last job title	Immediate supervisor	Title

Description of work and responsibilities

Which duties did you like most?

Which duties did you like least?

PREVIOUS EMPLOYMENT

Next previous employer	Address	Kind of business

Starting date Month / Year	Leaving date Month / Year	Starting pay	Final pay	Reason for leaving

Last job title	Immediate supervisor	Title

Description of work and responsibilities

Which duties did you like most?

Which duties did you like least?

I hereby swear that all of the above information is true to the best of my knowledge and any omission or falsification is grounds for my immediate dismissal.

DATE ______________ SIGNATURE ______________________

can do. Call your former employer and ask them to check their records and provide you with the information. If they refuse, go to the company with proper identification and *demand* they furnish the information. If they still refuse, report them to the Labor Department. *If the company is now out of business,* write "now out of business" for item 43—*neatly.* You are giving *information* and assisting the screener in not wasting time trying to locate the company.

At this point some of you are thinking, "I can't list some of my jobs; I will get bad references. " To begin straightening things out, you *must* list the jobs with bad references along with the good ones in proper order. Right after dealing with the numbered items, we will tell you how to make changes.

(47) Starting Pay and (48) Final Pay

Use a "$" (dollar sign) in front of each pay statement, and abbreviations for rate of pay, such as "wk." (week), "hr." (hour), "mo." (month). Thus eight hundred dollars per month would be $800.00/mo.; eight dollars per hour would be $8.00/hr. Do not forget the decimal points. Be complete and detailed here, too.

If they ask the starting pay and final pay, they want to see if you received pay raises for work well done, or merit increases. They cannot find out even on a reference check; 90 percent of employers will not release salary information without a release from you, the former employee. Small companies might give this information, but large companies will not.

(49) Reason for Leaving

- If you have been writing "Quit," change it to "Resigned."
- If you have been writing "Layoff" or, "Laid off," change it to "Reduction in force." (This indicates that more than one person was laid off due to circumstances *not* in your control.)

- If you resigned to return to school, say "Resigned to return to school."
- If you were terminated for cause or fired... *wait!* The instructions for handling what you write in that case will be explained after we finish the numbered items.
- If you moved from the area, say "Moved from area."
- If the company folded, moved or management changed hands, say "Company went out of business" or "Company moved" or "Change in management."

(50) May We Contact?

This question is to protect you on a reference check if you are still working. It is not professional for a prospective employer to call a present employer unless the applicant approves. Many times, your current employer is aware you are looking for work and is willing to give you a good recommendation. But if you are changing jobs and the prospective employer calls your current employer who is unaware of your plans, you could easily be *looking for a job* instead of *changing jobs!*

(51) Present or Last Job Title

This is self-explanatory. What was it? Do not attempt to pad or elevate your position by using titles you decided to give yourself. Throughout the United States there are scores of job titles in business and government that, basically, mean the same thing... but some *sound* "grander" than others. Naturally, you pick *that* one. Do not. This tactic can be too easily exposed during a reference check of a former employer where information is freely given.

(52) Immediate Supervisor

Give the person's name. If he or she is still employed there (call and check on it without talking with them at this point) put down the name. If the first name is not known, use "Mr.," "Mrs." or "Ms." followed by the last name.

IF THERE WAS A PERSONALITY CLASH RESULTING IN THAT PERSON DISMISSING YOU OR FORCING YOU TO RESIGN, OR IF YOU 'WALKED OUT' ON THEM, DO NOT PUT THE NAME IN YET. You will receive instructions on pages 61–64 for handling these problems.

If the individual is no longer working for the company, do not put the name in. Write "No longer with co./personnel."

Write in the area code and the telephone number of the company for each job right above the name. If the application has a space for this, fine. If it does not and you provide the telephone number for each job, the screener of the applications will be dazzled by your *providing* the information. Phone numbers of local firms can be obtained from the telephone directory or Information. Numbers for jobs you had in another town can be obtained by dialing the area code followed by 555-1212. The Information operator will give you the number *and* if you ask, will give you the address as well. *You* look up the Zip Code. If you can't afford the dollar and some for a Zip Code book, call the post office for all the zip codes you need for the entire application, where addresses are called for. *You must provide this detailed information.*

(53) Supervisor's Title

Give the title assigned your supervisor by the company, or just write "Supervisor." You can always ask the company for the specific title.

(54) Description of Work and Responsibilities

Just list key duties here because you are going to have a resume by the time you finish reading this book. The resume will contain the details of the duties. But *never* say in this space "See resume." Complete this space anyway. Why? Because they asked you to. You are showing that you know how to follow instructions, and they will be impressed or, to use the word I've mentioned before, dazzled by your skill in handling detail.

(55) Which duties did you like most?

List several key duties, whether or not you liked them.

(56) Which duties did you like least?

Do not list *any* duties here. Write "None." But don't write this for all the previously held jobs you've listed. It is unlikely and unbelievable that you did not have any duties you did not like in *all* your jobs. The trick here is to avoid citing specific duties. Some change-of-pace answers are:

JOB ENVIRONMENT [harmless]

POOR EQUIPMENT [likely]

Suppose you do list specific duties you did not like. How do you know that particular duty is not some part of the job for which you are now applying? You don't. *They do,* and your answer can immediately screen you *out!*

Using the numbered guide on the application work sheet and following these instructions, complete your work history. If you had more jobs than there is room for on the application, your resume will state the rest. It's the most recent jobs that are the most important.

a. How to handle bad references

The first step is this: You *must* phone *all* of your former supervisors. It makes no difference if:

- You *know* you will get a *good* reference. You will be refreshing their memory of you so that they are prepared for a call from a prospective employer checking your reference. That way, during busy work hours, they will not have to fumble for who you were and what you did. Do not depend on that "letter of reference"—the prospective employer will call anyway.

- You *know* you will get a *bad* reference. Unless you injured your former supervisor [or threatened to], or were involved in material or money theft, you can count on a very high forgive-and-forget factor. But to trigger that factor, you are going to have to swallow your pride. Here is how you do it:

> *Get your former supervisor who terminated you on the phone.* Hello Mr./Mrs./Ms.__________, this is__________. I worked for you in__________, doing__________. I was terminated by you for (insert exactly what they told you at the time)__________. I admit that during that period I did not have my act together and was not a good employee, but I have grown a lot since that time. [or] I now see the errors I made more clearly and am determined to change my attitude. While I know that professionally I cannot count on you for a good reference, could you do me a favor if a prospective employer calls you and verify only the dates I worked for you without mentioning any negative parts of my employment? I really need this from you to get a job and get on the right track.

This will work 95 percent of the time. Don't compromise on making this speech and let your pride get in the way. You will never regret it. The skills you had on the job won't be wasted or lost, and there won't be a gap because you were afraid of what they would say. In our workshop setting, once we convinced people to get on the phone and do this and they saw it work, the relief they experienced was awesome. The first call will be the hardest if you blew more than one job and have to make other similar calls.

Should your former supervisor refuse to cooperate, you have two more options:

- If that company has a personnel department, *go there* and ask them what information is given during a check. They will tell you. If what they give is merely date hired/left (and this is all a *personnel department* will usually give unless the checking company has a signed release from *you* to give more), then instead of the supervisor's name, write "Personnel" and its phone number in box 52.

- If personnel will also disclose why you were terminated, perhaps you should eliminate that job from your records *unless:*

You write in box 49 (reason for leaving):
"Will discuss in interview."

If you choose this route instead of eliminating the job altogether at the application stage, you will be beating the bad reference to the punch, since references are not checked until *after* the interview. Then *during the interview,* when you *will be* asked to discuss the matter, you must avoid the specific reasons and state to the interviewer that:

a. I had a personality conflict with my supervisor—I don't know why, it just happened.... It probably was *both* of our faults.
b. I felt the job had been misrepresented and I did not know how to deal with it at the time, so I reacted badly, but I have grown as a result.
c. At the time I had personal problems that kept me from performing to the best of my ability. Those have been solved and I am now able to make a positive contribution to a company.

Do not place the blame for your dismissal entirely on the employer, even if deserved. You are probably aware that a, b or c *really* are the causes for your being fired, regardless of the specific incidents that triggered the termination. We found these three reasons to be the most common causes for dismissal for most of our participants who had termination problems. Stating them in the way we have suggested above doesn't make them sound so bad, does it? If, during the reference check, the former supervisor or personnel person reacts emotionally about your termination or performance, you have already *logically* stated the reason there was a problem on the job. You have indicated a human weakness in yourself that has *obviously been corrected through your growth and coming to grips with yourself.* These honest admissions, together with a *dazzlingly detailed application, a resume that sells your skills, and an interview giving employers the right answers* will reduce the impact of a bad reference and get you the offer.

b. How to handle gaps between jobs

If, during any period between jobs you did *anything* on your own to bring in money, that effort qualifies you to state "Self-employed" in box 43 on the application, for that period when you were not working for someone else. You are telling the truth. What you did can be discussed in an interview and avoids leaving that period of time that you did not *work* for someone else blank. If what you did [full- or part-time] was related to the work you are seeking, it keeps you from appearing "skills stale." Attending school for anything in any subject—no matter how many hours per week—qualifies you to place "Attended school" in box 43. Again, you are telling the truth. It looks better if you were taking a course or courses that relate to the work you seek. But if the courses were *un*related, just state during the interview that you wanted to take yourself away from work for a period to explore new directions. If you were needed at home during a family illness or other crisis, particularly an economic crisis, state in box 43, "Attending to family matters." Be prepared, of course, to discuss the crisis in an interview.

If you were loafing around or could not find work, prepare your resume as in resume sample 14, with a summary of your skills in short form and an *undated* list of employers in order to get yourself through the doorway. Complete the application, leaving the gaps, and simply state in the interview that you could not find work during that period. Your application, resume and answers to the interview questions will impress the employer so that he will not be overly concerned about why you did not work during a certain period or periods. The thank-you letter we are going to teach you to write will punch it home. Besides, no one will even question your not being able to find work, with so many millions of people out of work and millions more too discouraged to look in this recession economy. The point is to appear, by your presentation, "work-ready" to the employer.

c. *A special word to the ex-offender*

If, during incarceration, you were assigned to a work detail that held a name other than that of the actual detention facility, place the name of that detail assignment in space 43 of the application for employer's name. Many areas, in order not to alarm the surrounding community by using "convicts" and other alarming names, use disguised, or less "threatening" names for the outside work details. If you were in one, you remember the name of it, we are sure. Use that name only on the application and resume. The detention facility *address* can still be used. You must get through the doorway and avoid being "screened out" because the detention facility name is recognizable to an application screener. Once in, during the interview, you must conform to the rules of your probation/parole by stating that you have a conviction record. We have found that 90 percent of your probation or parole officers require you to state your status to an employer. During the interview you simply say: "I must tell you that I have a conviction record, BUT I RECEIVED EXCELLENT COUNSELING AND WORK EXPERIENCE AND I AM FULLY PREPARED AND ANXIOUS TO JOIN PRODUCTIVE SOCIETY AND MAKE A CONTRIBUTION." Again, you must swallow your pride to do this and overcome your embarrassment. It is hard only the *first* time. If you are still rejected, keep doing it. If you are sincere and come across that way, you will soon find a job. We have seen it happen time and again—even for those who have committed serious crimes. If you are rejected, instead of reacting negatively, make a point of studying the reaction of the interviewers to your statement and learn to adjust the manner and wording with which you state your past until you are comfortable, project sincerity and learn to judge why or how you turn off the interviewer. When you get the job, word will probably spread that you are an ex-offender. Refuse to discuss any aspect of your past with fellow workers, and do not react to others who have a morbid curiosity about your past. Prove yourself on the job. You will never regret this approach once you get a job.

For married women, displaced homemakers and single parents entering or reentering the job market: Place "Homemaker" in box 43 and the dates in box 46. This will indicate that you are following instructions about accounting for time and will not raise questions, at this stage of applying, about a gap.
Students: Place "Attending school" in box 43 and the dates in box 46.

These tips on rebuilding your bridges and dealing with gaps will keep you from being screened out at the application stage. Following the instructions on how to use them will help you to avoid losing the self-esteem that comes from the frustration of not knowing how to deal with your past mistakes. Nothing we recommend here is illegal or deceptive, providing you follow the instructions exactly and deal with any past mistakes you may have made. You now have the opportunity and know-how to correct these mistakes and start over again.

NOW RECOPY YOUR WORK SHEET DETAIL ONTO THE FOLLOWING MASTER COPY APPLICATION FORM. ONCE YOU HAVE DONE THIS, YOU HAVE THE "PERFECT" GUIDE FOR FILLING OUT APPLICATIONS.

BE VERY CAREFUL IN TRANSFERRING THIS INFORMATION ONTO OTHER FORMS. YOU WILL *NEVER* SEE AN APPLICATION JUST LIKE THE ONE YOU HAVE COMPLETED, BUT WE HAVE COVERED ALL LEGAL AND ILLEGAL POSSIBILITIES YOU MAY COME ACROSS. YOU MUST TRANSFER THE INFORMATION IN COMPLETE DETAIL FOR THE "DAZZLE" FACTOR AND ULTIMATE SELECTION FOR AN *INTERVIEW*.

NOW YOU ARE READY TO LEARN HOW TO PREPARE A RESUME TO GO WITH THE APPLICATION. These are the two basic tools that will get you that interview.

C. PREPARING A RESUME: DOING IT THE EASY WAY WITH A RESUME WORK SHEET

The mere thought of preparing a resume frustrates everyone from those with less than an eighth-grade education to those with advanced degrees. Why? Several reasons. It is hard to settle on a format, what to say first and how to compose the resume in proper business language. It is difficult to understand that *every* skill you have ever learned on any job is *important* and *significant.* Most people pick out only the "highlight" skill and think that if they mention others, this will detract from the skill most identified with what they are seeking. Many people just do not

d. *Master copy of the application for employment*

(MASTER COPY) APPLICATION FOR EMPLOYMENT (1) Date ____________

VITAL INFORMATION, HIDDEN MEANINGS AND ILLEGAL QUESTIONS Print only, use pencil.

(2) Type of work desired ____________ (3) Social Security no. ____________

(4) Name ____________
LAST FIRST MIDDLE (MAIDEN NAME IF MARRIED)

(5) Birthdate ________ (6) Height ________ (7) Weight ________ (8) Phone ________

(9) Present address ____________ City ____________ Zip Code ________

(10) How long have you lived at the above address? ____________

(11) Previous address ____________

(12) Salary required: $ ______ per ______ (13) When available to begin work? ____________

(14) Husband's or wife's name ____________ (15) Occupation ____________

(16) Number of children ________ Ages ____________

(17) Are you bondable? ____________

(18) General health: Poor ________ Fair ________ Good ________ Excellent ________

(19) Do you have any physical or health limitations? ________ If yes, describe ________
____

(20) Have you or any of your family been treated for an emotional or mental problem? ________
If yes, explain ____________

(21) Have you ever received workmen's compensation? ____________

(22) How many days of work or school have you missed in the past year? ____________

(23) Military status ____________ If veteran, when inducted ____________
Branch ________ Date discharged ________ Type of discharge ________

(24) Have you been convicted of a crime on or after your 18th birthday? ____________
If yes, give date, nature and disposition ____________
____

(25) Languages spoken ____________ (26) Special talents ____________

(27) Do you plan any future schooling? ____________

(28) Interest in other work ____________

(29) Do you type? ________ (30) Take dictation? ________ (31)Operate office machines? ________
Specify ____________

(32) What are your interests or hobbies? ____________

(33) What clubs or organizations are you a member of? ____________

EDUCATION

(34) TYPE OF SCHOOL	(35) NAME OF SCHOOL	(36) LOCATION	(37) YEARS ATTENDED FROM MO./YR. TO MO./YR.	(38) GRADUATE YES NO	(39) DEGREE	(40) MAJOR OR COURSES	(41) GRADE POINT AVERAGE
HIGH SCHOOL				☐ ☐			
COLLEGE				☐ ☐			
GRADUATE SCHOOL				☐ ☐			
BUSINESS OR TRADE SCHOOL				☐ ☐			
MILITARY SCHOOLS				☐ ☐			
OTHER				☐ ☐			

REFERENCES

(42)
PLEASE LIST TWO PERSONAL REFERENCES WHOM WE MAY CONTACT—EXCLUDE RELATIVES

NAME ADDRESS TELEPHONE NUMBER YEARS KNOWN

NAME ADDRESS TELEPHONE NUMBER YEARS KNOWN

PRESENT or LAST EMPLOYMENT

PREVIOUS EMPLOYMENT RECORD

List former places of employment including temporary and permanent positions. Leave no lapse of time unaccounted for. Begin with present or most recent position.

Present or last employer (43)	Address (44)	Kind of business (45)

Starting date Month / Year	Leaving date Month / Year (46)	Starting pay (47)	Final pay (48)	Reason for leaving (49)	May we contact? (50)

Present or last job title (51)	Immediate supervisor (52)	Supervisor's title (53)

Description of work and responsibilities (54)

Which duties did you like most? (55)

Which duties did you like least? (56)

PREVIOUS EMPLOYMENT

Next previous employer	Address	Kind of business

Starting date Month / Year	Leaving date Month / Year	Starting pay	Final pay	Reason for leaving

Last job title	Immediate supervisor	Title

Description of work and responsibilities

Which duties did you like most?

Which duties did you like least?

Next previous employer	Address	Kind of business

Starting date Month / Year	Leaving date Month / Year	Starting pay	Final pay	Reason for leaving

Last job title	Immediate supervisor	Title

Description of work and responsibilities

Which duties did you like most?

Which duties did you like least?

PREVIOUS EMPLOYMENT

Next previous employer	Address	Kind of business

Starting date Month / Year	Leaving date Month / Year	Starting pay	Final pay	Reason for leaving

Last job title	Immediate supervisor	Title

Description of work and responsibilities

Which duties did you like most?

Which duties did you like least?

I hereby swear that all of the above information is true to the best of my knowledge and any omission or falsification is grounds for my immediate dismissal.

DATE ____________ SIGNATURE ____________________

understand that it is necessary to brag when job-seeking. We brag in *nonthreatening social settings,* but during a job search many people clam up. Start thinking of the word "brag" in terms of the word *"sell."* That should help as we go along. The only time you can get away with bragging *is* during a job search. If you do not brag (sell), your competition is going to and will most likely be a finalist for the position. And these days a resume is an *absolute requirement* if you are going to be competitive.

1. FOR THOSE WITH A COLLEGE EDUCATION

The resume is not supposed to be a literary triumph; it is a *sales tool,* nothing more. We have seen resumes from college grads so garbled with "school terms" that businesspeople cannot identify with any aspect of their abilities. This is understandable because the language of *school* is not the language of *business.* So if someone just leaving school has no work experience, the only terms he or she knows how to use are those of school settings. The resume becomes a test paper to impress the reader with the writer's *knowledge* rather than a brief description of skills that have practical application in business.

Pity the poor screener who has to read these resumes. Some applicants take the attitude that their resumes (like their applications) are the only ones received and design them to be published rather than read. And they also assume that because they are college-educated, their education, alone and highlighted on the resume, makes them the prime candidates for the position. A perfectly capable college graduate soon becomes discouraged and baffled because he or she was not selected for an interview based on the submission of a literary triumph of a resume.

2. FOR THOSE WITH A HIGH SCHOOL EDUCATION OR LESS

If you are going for a warehouse job, a kitchen-help job, a gardening job, a clerical job, a computer-training job, *any* job—you need a resume. Even if you have listed your skills on an application, the mere fact that you *have* a resume will help you to compete. Because you think it is difficult, you place little importance on developing one. We understand. That is why we are going to make it as simple as possible for you to develop one.

There are many books published just on the subject of resumes. We know. We have a complete reference library on the subject. These books often contradict one another and confuse the reader. Which style? What to include? What not to include? How to word them? These books give good advice, but they're presented so "you don't get it."

The *simpler resume is better* for the person who has to *read* it. Some people, realizing they must have a resume, slap it together in haphazard style, misspell, and abuse it physically, so it is presented looking as though they had slept on it.

As part of your Employment Package, we are going to make composing your resume as simple as possible without running you through a course in English grammar or boring you with terms such as "action verbs," "words that sell" or a course in English composition.

3. CHRONOLOGICAL AND FUNCTIONAL RESUMES

A *chronological* resume lists your jobs exactly as they appear on your application. They must *match.* The listing is by month and year of each job, starting with the present or last job first.

A *functional* approach calls attention to your skills in the beginning and may or may not include an undated list of jobs in which these skills were used. We recommend an undated list.

We will help you construct a chronological resume using the format and language of the samples that follow this presentation. From the various blue- and white-collar-worker sample chronological resumes we have underlined key words you may use to precede your skills and create the most effective sentences for selling those skills briefly. To make your own statements, use the *skills* you listed on the master application form and the *words* we have underlined on the sample chronological resumes. If you cannot do this on your own, get help.

Sections 4 through 10 will show you how to prepare each section of a chronological resume. Section 11 is a resume work sheet which you can use in preparing your own resume. If you need another work sheet to use in preparing a second resume, please copy the pages of Section 11.

4. NAME, ADDRESS, OBJECTIVE

Name—self-explanatory Telephone: (area code) number
Address—self-explanatory Message: (area code) number
Objective

Have two objectives: One is your *primary* objective; the other is your *survival* objective. You should write a separate resume for each objective.

If you are not sure what to put as an objective *or* have a skill that is difficult to pin down with a job title, use an objective that states *no* specific job title. *Example: Seeking a position utilizing my work experience with an established firm offering advancement for measured achievement.* If you are following instructions for applying for a job where only a resume is requested by mail, call attention to the specific job in your cover letter. If you are sending an application, the job you are applying for will be on the application. If there is no space to say what job you are applying for, write it in at the top of the application in the upper right-hand corner.

By phrasing your objective in this way: (1) You have stated you are looking for an established firm in which you can grow and (2) you are willing to provide measured achievement for advancement. You have the right attitude. This way, when you finish your resume and you become aware of a job that fits your skills but not your specific objective, you do not have to rewrite or print a different resume for each job opening that fits your skills but not your stated objective. You are not "locked into" one title.

Use one resume to find out where you stand competitively in your first choice for a job, and the other to survive until you get what you really want, either by luck or by getting the skills you need via further education or on-the-job training.

5. EMPLOYMENT EXPERIENCE

List your work experience as it appears on your master application. List your last job *first,* up to a maximum of five jobs. That is the usual number of jobs provided for on most applications. Some have room for three only. AT THE END OF EACH JOB LISTING, DESCRIBE WHAT YOU DID AND TELL WHAT YOU ACCOMPLISHED IN THAT JOB. Did you improve efficiency? Say so by calling attention to a percentage of improvement. Did you do something on that job that indicated trust, such as "Opened and closed shop daily?" (You had a *key;* they trusted you, you were "responsible.") Did you do something on that job that no one before you did? Did you design a systems form for more efficiency? *Say so.* This is called *measuring a job.* And don't be shy about stating your achievements and responsibilities. But don't go overboard and overstate or inflate them, either.

6. EDUCATION

List the last school you attended or highest degree *first,* then all schools, in order, after that one, with high school listed *last.* If you have only a high school education, that is all you can place on the resume under education. Special trade schools, technical schools, real-estate schools, schooling in the military, social program training schools—*all* these should be listed in the date order you attended. *Any* schooling, even if unrelated to the job you are seeking, is important. If nothing else was learned, employers know you were exposed to social interaction and discipline. This can be interpreted by a screener as forward momentum, activity you pursued on your own.

7. REFERENCES

Furnished upon request. (This merely indicates that you are able to furnish professional references from past jobs or from people who know you personally.) After what you have learned in preparing your application, you should be confident in stating this.

8. FOR THOSE WHO CAN AFFORD TO HAVE SOMEONE PREPARE THEIR RESUME

Resume preparation services have become a big business because of people's inability to judge what type of resume they should have, much less how to prepare them. Look in the yellow pages under "Resumes." Having one prepared can run from very inexpensive [$10–$25] to *very* expensive [$25–$100], depending on the degree of difficulty in its preparation. Take your master application form to a resume service and get a quote. Tell them you want it prepared to match what is on the master application. They may ask additional questions about those job *skills* to improve the statement of each job description. Most resume services also provide printing services, either as part of the charge or for an extra charge.

9. FOR THOSE WHO CANNOT AFFORD A RESUME SERVICE

Ask a friend or relative to follow our instructions and assist you in preparing your resume. If you do it yourself, USE THE RESUME WORK SHEET FORM AND FOL-

LOW RESUME SAMPLE 2 IN THIS BOOK. USE OTHER SAMPLES WITH UNDERLINED WORDS TO PRECEDE YOUR JOB SKILLS TO MAKE SENTENCES OR STATEMENTS. PRINT. Then take this to a SECRETARIAL SERVICE (see the Yellow Pages) and have them type the master copy for you (at about $3–$4 per page). Then take the master copy to a "quickie" printing service and have them print it on white or off-white paper. (Don't get artsy and use colored paper, unless you have an "artsy" skill.) The total cost will run *under* $15.

For those who can't afford a secretarial service and a printing service

- Have a friend who types well do it for you, using your neatly printed form and our format sample from the book.
- Go to a large drugstore and use their copying machine (or ask a friend who has access to a copy machine and is willing to run them off for you).

Total cost: under $5 (and maybe a beer for the friend).

10. MAKING A JOB THAT SOUNDS LIKE NOTHING INTO SOMETHING

In a county in California that will remain nameless, the county sponsored a "roof rat program." Neighborhoods were having problems with roof rats, so the county killed two birds with one tax-dollar stone and hired CETA-eligible participants and used CETA federal tax dollars to establish a community service program called Rodent Control. This enabled the county to address the problem of roof rats and provide one-year employment for those qualified for CETA jobs. Some 55 people were employed to contact eligible homeowners and then get rid of the rats in their homes. It is probably the only time in history rats were involved in providing temporary jobs for the unemployed.

Most of those employed in the program went through our training after the roof rat program was completed, and we started preparing their resumes. Since the most recent job listed on a resume is usually the most important, we asked the group to list the skills they learned during this roof rat employment. One man said, "Man, there ain't no skills to crawling through attics and house foundations hanging bait!" It wasn't easy to translate this, but here's what we came up with:

> Assembled daily and split into work crews, were driven to work sites and unloaded work equipment. Accepted daily assignments from crew leader. Located areas where pests nested and dispensed bait to eliminate. Responsible for courteous treatment and cooperated with homeowner. Marked daily sheets and kept records of scheduled visits.

We changed a very demoralizing job of "hanging bait" into a job that included the following:

- Had to be at work on time (assembled to be driven to work sites)
- Worked individually and as part of a team (assembled, driven to job, crawled alone)
- Strong person (unloaded equipment)
- Sequential skills (used head to find rats)
- Customer service (courteous treatment/worked with owner)
- Record keeping (marked daily sheets/kept records)

The roof rat program was exceeded in the category of "jobs I wished I hadn't had" only by the "weed abatement program," where scores of Vietnam veterans slashed weeds all day for a year. Needless to say, those who made it through the year were not in either the best mood or state of job-readiness when they got to our program. But, you see, you can make something out of practically nothing to indicate skills.

11. THE RESUME WORK SHEET

THIS FORM FOLLOWS RESUME SAMPLE 2. FOLLOW THE INSTRUCTIONS WE HAVE GIVEN YOU IN FILLING IT OUT CAREFULLY. FOR PLACING ADDITIONAL INFORMATION ON YOUR RESUME, CHOOSE ONE OF THE OTHER RESUME FORMATS AND REVIEW HOW IT WAS CONSTRUCTED.

WORK SHEET

NAME RESUME

Street address Telephone ( ) ________
City, state, Zip Code Message ( ) ________

OBJECTIVE

EMPLOYMENT EXPERIENCE (List last job *first*, then the job before that, etc.)

Date from–Date to Name of firm ________
City ________ Zip Code ____
Your job title ________
(Description) ________
____
____
____

Date from–Date to Name of firm ________
City ________ Zip Code ____
Your job title ________
(Description) ________
____
____
____

Date from–Date to	Name of firm ________________ City __________________ Zip Code _____ Your job title __________________ (Description) ________________________ ______________________________________ ______________________________________ ______________________________________
Date from–Date to	Name of firm ________________ City __________________ Zip Code _____ Your job title __________________ (Description) ________________________ ______________________________________ ______________________________________ ______________________________________
Date from–Date to	Name of firm ________________ City __________________ Zip Code _____ Your job title __________________ (Description) ________________________ ______________________________________ ______________________________________ ______________________________________
EDUCATION	Name of college ____________________ City/state _____________ Zip Code _____ Degree obtained ____________________
	Name of high school ________________ City/state _____________ Zip Code _____
	Other schooling, such as trade school, military, etc.
REFERENCES	Furnished upon request.

12. RESUME SAMPLES

There are two groups: Blue-collar-job resume samples and white-collar-job resume samples.

We have underlined key words you can place before your skill listings. This keeps you from constantly using "*I* did this" or "*I* did that." We have underlined descriptive words as well as action words. Borrow freely from the language in these resumes. They worked for others, and they will work for you. *Notice how simple and easy to read they are.*

For blue-collar workers: If you showed up even at a gas station for a job and had a resume, you would beat out the competition for the job as long as you were basically qualified. And if you write a thank-you letter and drop it off afterward, the person doing the hiring would be so impressed that the other applicants wouldn't stand a chance against you. (More on thank-you letters later in the book.)

For all of you: Note how the following resumes state skills that *you* might consider unimportant or unsalable. You may assume that because you are "good" in "very impressive" skills, the "little ones" will be taken for granted. *No way.* List *all* your skills, starting with the most impressive and ending up with the little ones. Every piece of equipment or machinery you operate must be listed. Blue-collar workers should name the equipment and power tools they operate and "lump" the hand/manual tools into one category. For example, "Operate McCullough Chain Saw, Hyster forklift, Black & Decker power drill and small hand tools." If you do not operate power tools, *list* the hand tools and equipment you can use.

For white-collar workers: List everything *but* desktop items—staple remover, hole punch, etc. This would be interpreted as "padding." We've seen this too much not to mention it.

Each resume for both blue-collar and white-collar jobs has been numbered. Below, by resume number, we tell you a few things about the people behind these resumes other than their skills, and follow with the resume itself. Arrows on the resume enable you to locate quickly what we are talking about. The underlined words and arrows are for your help *only.* Do not use them on *your* resume.

a. Blue-collar-job resumes

1. *Warehousing*

We listed the military experience *first;* it was a *paid* job. There was no extensive warehousing experience since 1976, and the person did other things as well in the military. However, the warehousing experience in the military kept the resume from looking "stale" between 1976 and 1979.

RESUME SAMPLE 1

JOHN JOB SEEKER — RESUME

3333 Third Street — Telephone (415)333-3333
Jobsville, CA 33333 — Messages (415)233-1111

OBJECTIVE — Seeking a warehousing position utilizing my background in shipping and receiving.

MILITARY EXPERIENCE

May 1977–November 1979 — United States Marine Corps
Camp Pendleton, San Diego, CA
Private First Class

⇨ Served as *warehouseman/supply personnel, baker* and *combat engineer.* As a warehouseman, I pulled and filled incoming requisitions and operated both battery and gasoline engine forklifts. As a baker, I prepared a wide range of foods, such as bread, cake, puddings, pies, etc.

EMPLOYMENT EXPERIENCE

November 1976– May 1977		Perkin-Elmer Corporation Mountain View, CA *Machine Operator*
		Responsible for checking all machinery and parts (i.e., pumps, generators) for leaks. After visual inspection, utilized leak tester for further checking. When leak located and analyzed, would then have welder eliminate it.
May 1976– October 1976		Velo-Bind Incorporated (bookbinders) Sunnyvale, CA *Warehouseman*
		Pulled and filled invoices; kept up warehouse inventories. Wrapped, loaded and unloaded, utilizing forklift where necessary and performed light maintenance. Responsible for all outgoing letters and packages, making sure they had correct postage for their mailing class, were correctly wrapped and were distributed to the correct company. Provided all drivers with proper instructions for delivery.

EDUCATION

September 1977– December 1977		Marine Corps Baking School San Diego, CA
January 1976–		3M Truck Driving School

April	1976	San Francisco, CA Class I, II, III driving license; diesel operations, CVC inspections
September June	1971– 1975	Carlmont High School Belmont, CA General education, basic shop, woodwork

---

2. *Gardening*

This man was smart, but he dropped out. He couldn't handle confinement. He liked to work outdoors. We discovered what he really wanted to do and convinced him he would have to return to school first. In the meantime he had to survive and, because he could do the things we listed in "self-employment," he chose gardening. It also kept him outside.

RESUME SAMPLE 2

JOHN JOB SEEKER	RESUME
3333 Third Street Jobsville, CA 33333	Telephone (415) 333-3333 Messages (415) 233-1111

OBJECTIVE — Seeking a position with an established firm utilizing my background in the field of landscape gardening.

EMPLOYMENT EXPERIENCE

March Present	1978–	Self-employed Colma, CA *Gardener*
	⇨	Operate own business. Prune bushes and trees. Plant flowers, weed areas

and blow away leaves and debris. Map out garden paths and plan sprinkler systems. Prepare ground for new lawns, plant and maintain lawns. Bill customers and make collections. Familiar with soils, tools, fertilizers, planting, mowers, tree trimming and seasonal planting.

August February	1973– 1978	De Soto Sedan Company San Francisco, CA *Driver* Transported people throughout the San Francisco area. Maintained car and kept it in top mechanical condition.
September July	1967– 1973	United States Post Office San Francisco, CA *Mail-Baggage Handler* Cased mail, handled baggage. Was familiar with virtually every mail operation carried out in the Rincon annex.
March August	1966– 1967	Self-employed San Mateo Area, CA *Land Surveyor* Working out of the Surveyor's Union in San Mateo, performed surveying jobs for various highway contractors, subdividers and grading firms. Working from blueprints and maps, checked land elevations, extent of cut and fill needed and exact locations of construction projects. Determined boundaries of lots and blocks, streets

		and sidewalks. Utilized transit, level, rod and chain.
September July	1956– 1966	City and County of San Francisco San Francisco, Millbrae, CA *Rod and Chainman/Land Surveyor/ Inspector*
		Measured land, buildings, streets and property lines. Surveyed sites for dams. Established sewer and drainage routes so that they would go along downhill slopes. As inspector, examined steel, concrete structures. Worked as land surveyor for the San Francisco Water Department out of Millbrae for three years, mapping lines for water mains. Final four years were with the City Engineering Department, where, as a rod and chainman, I inspected sites and related structures and measured land and elevations, as well as slopes.
September February	1956– 1957	Kern County Land and Cattle Company Bakersfield, CA *Rod and Chainman*
		Checked level of ground so that land sloped properly for irrigation and canal work as well as protecting underground oil pipe lines.

EDUCATION

Summers	1955 & 1956	Bakersfield College Bakersfield, CA Psychology, languages

September	1946–	San Francisco City College
June	1949	San Francisco, CA
		Psychology, languages
September	1942–	High School of Commerce
June	1946	San Francisco, CA
		Science

REFERENCES Furnished upon request.

---

3. *Part-time office work*

No paid experience. Rural minority youth 17 years old. We summarized her personal traits as well as her sequential skills at home and her interests.

RESUME SAMPLE 3
NO PAID WORK EXPERIENCE

JUDY JOB SEEKER RESUME

3333 Third Street
Jobsville, CA 33333

Telephone (209) 333-3333

SUMMARY

⇨ Responsible young woman working hard on a volunteer basis at home to gain work experience skills that will enable me to seek a position as a part-time office worker. Follow instructions well, like to complete work assignments, work independently as well as with others and am eager to learn additional skills.

VOLUNTEER EXPERIENCE

January 1977–present

V. Avina
Lindsay, CA
Home Care Assistant

Assist parents with child care and household chores. Prepare food, wash dishes, keep rooms clean by vacuuming, dusting and polishing. Provide care for other children in family. Feed them, direct their play, discipline them when necessary and change their clothing.

SPECIAL SKILLS AND INTERESTS

Awarded ribbons in crafts for jewelry and ceramics.
Participate in gardening activities, working with vegetables and flowers.
Student aide in elementary school working with students in art activities.

EDUCATION

September 1979–present

Lindsay High School
Lindsay, CA
General education

REFERENCES Furnished upon request.

---

4. *General goal*

Inner-city black youth. Highlight of resume is vocational exploration/job search program as well as "volunteer work."

RESUME SAMPLE 4
CHRONOLOGICAL/VOLUNTEER WORK

JOHN JOB SEEKER RESUME

3333 Third Street Telephone (415) 333-3333
Jobsville, CA 33333

SUMMARY

Responsible youth with both sales and construction skills. Have 3.3 grade point average in high school. Have shown my ability to work with people, to be dependable and enthusiastic. I follow instructions and like to complete any job I have started.

EMPLOYMENT EXPERIENCE

June 1980– August 1980

Edna Foundation
East Palo Alto, CA
Employment Trainee

A seven-week program developing work-related behavior and attitudes. Upgraded job-ready skills, including verbal and written communication, problem solving, and decision making, organization of work, planning, motivation and goals. Prepared and organized numerous records and forms. Improved telephone, interview and public-speaking techniques. Researched various vocational fields and clarified personal goals. Upgraded knowledge of employee obligations, including punctuality, dependability and productivity.

General Assistant, Materials Department

Spent final two weeks as a general assistant with the materials department at Syntex Corporation in Palo Alto. Opened and packed incoming and outgoing shipments, placed inventory on the shelves and made complete records of shipments.

January 1979– June 1979		*Palo Alto Times* Palo Alto, CA *Newsboy* Delivered a route of 65 papers six days a week. Collected bills from subscribers the first of every month. Once a week, I solicited a designated territory for new subscriptions. Won a Ping-Pong table and wristwatch for being a top salesman.

VOLUNTEER WORK

May 1980– June 1980	Assisted friend and his father in building addition to home, utilizing drill, Skilsaw, bandsaw and hand tools.
March 1980– May 1980	Assisted uncle occasionally in his position as new-car sales manager at Arata Pontiac in Burlingame.
July 1979– August 1979	Assisted uncle in his fast-food restaurant in Fresno. Served customers hamburgers, fries and milkshakes.

EDUCATION

September 1979– present	Woodside High School Redwood City, CA

General education—art metal shop (making jewelry, bracelets), wood shop; wired sound equipment for concert.

REFERENCES Furnished upon request.

---

5. *Warehousing-related work*

Ex-offender. First two jobs listed were done in jail. Notice the use of "San Mateo County" and "State of California" to disguise prison term identification. In the interview, this person told the interviewer about this and followed up with positive statements about his rehabilitation. His attitude and presentation to the company enabled him to be hired. Remember, the idea is to *get* the interview. We deliberately omitted two dates in this resume to protect the identity of the individual.

RESUME SAMPLE 5
CHRONOLOGICAL

JOHN JOB SEEKER RESUME

3333 Third Street Telephone (415) 333-3333
Jobsville, CA 33333 Messages (415) 233-1111

OBJECTIVE Seeking a position in the field of warehousing, or related work, with an established firm offering advancement for measured achievement.

EMPLOYMENT EXPERIENCE

January 1980–present ⇨ San Mateo County
San Mateo, CA
Warehouseman Trainee

Worked in stock room, handing out kitchen and laundry supplies, as well as performed kitchen duties. Unloaded trucks, helped stack boxes in proper places. Learned warehousing procedures, including clerical requirements.

January December	1979– 1979	State of California Nevada City, CA *Fire Fighter*
		Assisted in fire-fighting operations in the Sierra foothills, working out of the Washington Ridge Conservation Camp, Forestry Division. Skills utilized included operation of chain saw, backfiring and brush cutting. Participated in search parties, saved several lives, retrieved bodies.
May December	1977– 1978	Manpower Palo Alto, CA *Warehouseman*
		Loaded trucks and stacked boxes, with incidental operation of electric forklifts, in temporary positions for various local firms, particularly the Commodore Corporation of Palo Alto.
June March		Bailey Security San Jose, CA *Security Guard*
		Guarded against fire, theft, vandalism and illegal entry. Patrolled beat, checked doors and windows to insure their being secure. Warned violators of rule infractions, such as loi-

tering, smoking and carrying forbidden articles; kept out unauthorized persons.

EDUCATION

June September	Ravenswood High School East Palo Alto, CA General education; wood shop
REFERENCES	Furnished upon request.

---

6. *Printing*

Very complete descriptions, indicating excellent knowledge of printing, quality control and use of equipment.

RESUME SAMPLE 6

JOHN JOB SEEKER	RESUME
3333 Third Street Jobsville, CA 33333	Telephone (415) 333-3333 Messages (415) 233-1111

OBJECTIVE	Seeking a position with an established firm in the field of printing.

EMPLOYMENT EXPERIENCE

October January	1979– 1980	Spearman Printing Menlo Park, CA *Print Shop Lead*
		Supervised small print shop, with a crew of six craftsmen. Responsibilities included taking in print orders, pricing jobs, planning daily schedule for each employee, supervising trainees on shop procedures and safety awareness, meeting deadlines

on orders and purchasing necessary supplies. Operated press, typesetting or any other equipment when necessary. Did emergency trouble-shooting when equipment broke down. Kept up inventory records and took care of any other production and administrative functions as needed.

October 1978–
October 1979

Alameda County Sheriff and Fire Marshal
Pleasanton, CA
Print Shop Lead-Trainer

Successfully trained and managed crew of 15 workers in the various skills needed to operate a print shop, including press operation, typesetting, layout and clerical. Organized operation so that job orders were completed with greatest efficiency and on time.

July 1972–
September 1978

State of California
Fairfield, CA
Control Clerk I (Procurement)

Responsible for procuring medical supplies, food, clothing, maintenance supplies and certain specialized supplies such as those needed for grinding optical lenses. Controlled accounts to ensure that no purchase be made unless there were adequate funds in the proper accounts so no account would be overdrawn. Organized centralized filing system to improve efficiency of operation. Delegated contracts to proper control clerks, saw that clerks followed through on back-order forms and purchase orders. Responsible for typing statistics and reports and for general office maintenance.

September	1967–	King's Kup Restaurant
March	1972	Alameda, CA
		Owner

Maintained own books and payroll records in 180-customer restaurant, keeping inventory records on food and beverages, recruiting, hiring and firing employees, planning entertainment, servicing equipment, supplying own janitorial service, scheduling weekly job sheets, maintaining successful public relations with customers. Even kept bar at times and led own musical group.

EDUCATION

June	1973–	Long Beach State University
July	1976	Long Beach, CA
		Business management
March	1964–	U.S. Navy
September	1964	U.S.S. *Hancock*
		Supply Clerk course
June	1958	Sunset High School
July	1962	Hayward, CA

SKILLS

Have operated the 1250/1275 Multi-Offset Press, the ABD-360 Radarstate Mark II Camera, Veritype

	Headliner, Plate Master Maker as well as various other types of printing equipment.
REFERENCES	Furnished upon request.

---

b. White-collar-job resumes

7. *General objective*

Note the way the objective is aimed. This approach allows her to be considered for either a government position or a job in private industry, without committing her to a specific job objective. Her goal in private business would be in customer/employee service-related jobs. Her background is exclusively social-service oriented.

RESUME SAMPLE 7

JUDY JOB SEEKER	RESUME
3333 Third Street Jobsville, CA 33333	Telephone (415) 333-3333 Messages (415) 233-1111

OBJECTIVE ⇨	Seeking a position with an established firm or agency to utilize my background in helping people with a wide range of problems.

EMPLOYMENT EXPERIENCE

March 1979–Present	Neighborhood Services Center South San Francisco, CA *Supervisor of Social Services*
	Refer and inform residents of resources in area. Listen to clients'

problems, advise them and decide whether they should receive emergency assistance. Plan and organize workshop for women and minorities in nontraditional employment. Develop food program for low-income families. Supervise two employees in social services and develop volunteer caseload for agency. Maintain follow-up system.

August 1977– September 1978	Division of Youth and Family Services Trenton, NJ *Social Worker* Placed abused children in day-care programs and followed up on their progress. Managed caseload of 75 families of inner-city residents. Used sensitivity and listening skills to confront and counsel clients. Observed family situations, investigated complaints of child abuse and neglect, evaluated day-care homes, prepared and calculated budget reviews of parents.
August 1977– September 1978	Office of Child Abuse Control Trenton, NJ *Social Worker* Answered "hot line" telephone. Served as referral source and counseled clients over telephone, recorded information, determined and assessed situations and decided whether an emergency worker should be sent to the home.

March	1975–	Division of Mental Retardation
August	1977	Trenton, NJ
		Social Worker
		Assigned case management of 115 clients. Solely responsible for placing disabled clients in private facilities throughout country. Analyzed case records, determined where client would be best suited, placed client. Evaluated private facilities, wrote reports on facilities and client's progress. Counseled parents during annual home visits.

EDUCATION

January	1973–	Trenton State College
December	1974	Trenton, NJ
		B.A. in sociology, social welfare; minor in psychology
September	1970–	Mercer County Community College
September	1972	Trenton, NJ
		Liberal arts
		Three semesters on dean's list
September	1966	Hamilton High West School
June	1970	Trenton, NJ

REFERENCES Furnished upon request.

---

8. *X-ray technologist*

This man spent his entire working life in prison, except for one most recent part-time position, which gave him credibility for practical application of what he learned and achieved in prison. It was necessary to highlight the education/skills he received in prison, including those listed under "Qualifications." We knew he would be questioned about the gaps, but the resume alone got him the interview, where he was able to explain his past, as required by his parole/probation officer. He was able to rejoin society in a job he enjoyed.

RESUME SAMPLE 8
CHRONOLOGICAL/FUNCTIONAL

JOHN JOB SEEKER — RESUME

3333 Third Street — Telephone (415) 333-3333
Jobsville, CA 33333 — Messages (415) 233-1111

OBJECTIVE	Seeking a position as an X-ray technologist.
EDUCATION	
June 1978– February 1980	State of California X-ray School Vacaville, CA State certificate: certified radiologic technologist
September 1973– January 1974	Hartnell College Salinas, CA Psychology, sociology, political science
September 1964– June 1967	Camp Hill High School Camp Hill (Harrisburg), PA General education, wood shop, sheet-metal shop, barbering (license)

EDUCATIONAL HIGHLIGHTS

State of California X-ray School—twenty months

X-ray technique	Anatomy
Physiology	Nursing
⇨ Physics	Radiation protection
Darkroom chemistry	Principles of radiography
Department administration	Ethics

QUALIFICATIONS	Am qualified to: Operate X-ray equipment under supervision of radiologists.
	Expose photographic plates of various parts of patient's bodies.
	Prepare barium salts and other opaque chemical substances in solution for ingestion by patients.
	Arrange proper shielding of patient to exposure of selected areas.
	Set controls of equipment for correct radiation dosage.
	Maintain medical X-ray treatment records.
	Assist radiologists in fluoroscopic exams.

PROFESSIONAL EXPERIENCE

May 1980–present	Half Moon Bay Community Hospital Moss Beach, CA *X-ray Technologist*
	As sole member of X-ray department during Saturdays and Sundays, I perform all duties. Also on call during evenings.

---

9. *Clerk-typist*

This woman, a single parent, received social-program training to brush up her clerical skills to reenter the job market. Note how all her skills are listed and defined.

RESUME SAMPLE 9

JUDY JOB SEEKER RESUME

3333 Third Street
Jobsville, CA 33333

Telephone (415) 333-3333
Messages (415) 233-1111

OBJECTIVE

Seeking a clerk-typist position with an established firm or agency offering advancement for measured achievement.

EMPLOYMENT EXPERIENCE

October 1979–present

Bay Area Urban League
South San Francisco, CA
Clerk-Typist Trainee

Type reports, business correspondence, menus, etc., as part of an on-the-job training program. Organized filing system, answer phones (six lines) on main call director, operate 10-key calculator, operate mag card.

September 1968–October 1979

Devoted full-time to being a homemaker and to rearing small children. Performed volunteer work (and continue to do so) for El Rancho School Library and El Rancho PTA as room mother and fund raiser.

August 1966–August 1968

Motel Five
Oakland, CA
Receptionist

Answered phone (three lines) on main call director. Greeted and handled customer complaints. Handled cash and did some typing and inventory work. Hotel had approximately 35 units.

EDUCATION

October 1979– April 1980		Opportunities Industrialization Center West South San Francisco, CA Clerical training
January 1975– June 1975		Skyline College San Bruno, CA Early childhood education
September 1962– June 1965		El Camino High School South San Francisco, CA General education, typing

REFERENCES Furnished upon request.

---

10. *Sales/marketing*

This resume includes good professional-position job descriptions, because each calls attention to the "success" factor and the applicant's contribution to the firm.

RESUME SAMPLE 10

JOHN JOB SEEKER RESUME

3333 Third Street
Jobsville, CA 33333

Telephone (415) 333-3333
Messages (415) 233-1111

OBJECTIVE

To obtain a position of responsibility within the public relations, marketing and/or financial organization of a major company, with the potential to move into general management.

EMPLOYMENT EXPERIENCE

November 1979–
August 1980

CPC Distributors, Inc.
San Leandro, CA
Marketing Consultant

Developed and devised marketing strategy that increased usage of Polyglycoat products within territorial limits. Held meetings designed to enlighten dealership personnel on the profitability of using Polyglycoat products, both individually and for the dealership as a whole.

November 1973–
October 1979

Kerwin-Austin Enterprises
San Carlos, CA
Marketing Sales Manager

Developed rapport with various real-estate brokers and investors. Determined most profitable investments in industrial and residential properties. Worked out successful advertising campaign, utilizing a mix of publications, which resulted in profitable sales of properties.

March 1970–
October 1973

Chrysler Motors Corporation/
Peugeot, Inc.
San Mateo, CA
District/Zone Sales Manager

Responsible for selling motor vehicles to Chrysler and Peugeot dealers. Successfully developed new franchise operation. Conducted sales seminars to keep dealership personnel constantly aware of the salable features of their vehicles. Analyzed dealers' financial statements and assisted them when necessary, making dealers aware of possible profit and/or loss situations. Developed marketing strategies that increased market penetration within the dealers' respective marketing areas. Conducted aggressive owner, customer and public-relations program to attain highest possible corporate and product reputation.

January March	1967– 1970	Kimberly, Inc. Los Angeles, CA *National Sales Manager*

Obtained competitive prices for mercury, then purchasing it, arranging for transportation, security, documentation and coordination of all aspects of mercury purchase agreements. This entailed extensive customer relations with existing accounts and development and acquisition of new business accounts. Increased sales approximately 220 percent. Helped devise new and profitable uses for mercury.

June September	1962– 1964	H. B. Fuller Company South San Francisco, CA *Sales Manager*

	Responsible for sale of industrial adhesives to major companies. Developed new uses for specialized products while working with a multiplicity of plant personnel. Developed new inroads into paper conversion and canning industries as well as maintaining customer relations with new and existing accounts.
EDUCATION	
September 1964– January 1967	Menlo College, School of Business Administration Atherton, CA B.S. in business administration, minor in accounting; Dean's list
January 1961– June 1962	Menlo College Atherton, CA Liberal arts
September 1960– January 1961	Monterey Peninsula College Monterey, CA Liberal arts
September 1956– June 1960	Woodside High School Redwood City, CA College prep
REFERENCES	Furnished upon request.

---

11. *Cook (service industries)*

Applicant is an ex-offender. Good cook/food services background. Note the use of underlined action words.

RESUME SAMPLE 11

JUDY JOB SEEKER — RESUME

333 Third Street
Jobsville, CA 33333
Telephone (415) 333-3333

OBJECTIVE

Seeking a position as a cook with an established firm or agency offering advancement for measured achievement.

EMPLOYMENT EXPERIENCE

May 1978–June 1980

State of California
Frontera, CA
Cook

Prepared all meals and special diets for a population of 1,300. I was in control of food preparation and all meals being put out by a specific time. Operated institutional-size steamers, steam pots and standard grills. Prepared all entrees, including salads, soups and special diets.

May 1977–July 1977

Sharon Heights Convalescent Hospital
Menlo Park, CA
Cook's Assistant/Pantry Aide

Arranged tray line, recognized and placed diets in proper area for serving. Assisted lead cook in all food preparation and special diet planning. Performed basic clean-up procedures around food-preparation area. Learned to prepare such diets as: bland, low-sodium, high-fiber, diabetic 1,000 and 1,200, puree, no-cholesterol, as well as portion control.

September 1976–
March 1977

Bayside Auto Dismantlers
San Francisco, CA
Auto Dismantler

Dismantled automobiles, operated light machinery such as forklifts and tow trucks. Took parts inventory, steam-cleaned all rebuilt engines and dismantled auto parts.

January 1975–
August 1976

Half Moon Bay Inn
Half Moon Bay, CA
Short-Order Cook

Did entire meal preparation, involving fast-food production. Worked with sauces. Put out three daily meals. Organized methods for the most efficient ways to put meals out quickly. Worked successfully under pressure, controlled all ordering for food preparation supplies. Utilized a variety of kitchen machinery, such as vegetable cutters, blenders, meal slicers and standard grills.

EDUCATION

September 1979–
June 1980

Laverne College
Laverne, CA
Biology, art

February 1973–
April 1976

South San Francisco High School
South San Francisco, CA
General education

REFERENCES Furnished upon request.

12. *Public/corporate communications*

The "Summary of Qualifications" was created to draw attention away from free-lancing and short-term positions and to emphasize the applicant's qualifications. The use of underlined words gives immediate accent to the applicant's strongest assets.

RESUME SAMPLE 12

JUDY JOB SEEKER	RESUMÈ
333 Third Street Jobsville, CA 33333	Telephone (415) 333-3333 Messages (415) 233-1111

OBJECTIVE

A position in public or corporate communications with emphasis on health/welfare, security and safety and the researching and analyzing of internal pragmatic affairs.

SUMMARY OF QUALIFICATIONS

Twenty years' experience in written communications, including public relations. Responsibilities and assignments have included the research, analyzing and reporting on business security, morale and humanistic behavior patterns. Other skills include promotion and promotion writing, research and development of criminal-justice planning and public safety as well as numerous contemporary assignments.

EMPLOYMENT EXPERIENCE

December 1978– December 1979	Redwood City Fire Department Redwood City, CA *Administrative Assistant*

Researched, analyzed and presented for evaluation programs to improve departmental performance. Assisted in preparation of ordinances for sprinkler systems and onsite construction. Coordinated fire-prevention programs for special groups such as seniors. Implemented programs for personnel to present to community.

1976–1978 *Consultant to:* Dr. Walter Gunn and Santa Cruz County.

For office of district attorney: Research consultant on rape, child molestation, jury selection practices.
For the courts: Special services—work furlough program.
For office of sheriff: Specialized in rape victims, witnesses and suspects.

FREE-LANCE PROJECTS
1955–1976

- Assisted in revision of SWAT Training Manual; created analysis and delivered presentation for segment of congressional investigation on SWAT in Santa Cruz County, CA.
- Consulted with AFT (Alcohol, Firearms and Tobacco) and Federal Narcotics Bureau on community-related problems associated with same.
- Associated within management for such firms as Marine World Africa USA, Marriott, Disneyland Hotel, city of Pacific Grove, city of Foster City and assignments for private attorneys.

- Investment consultant for real estate and property management.

EDUCATION	
1974–	Golden Gate University San Francisco, CA M.P.A. in public administration
1972–1974 Continuing ed.	Monterey Institute of Foreign Studies Monterey, CA Spanish
1973–1977 Continuing ed.	San Jose State University San Jose, CA Social welfare
1971–1978 Continuing ed.	University of California at Pomona, San Diego and Santa Cruz, CA Social welfare
EXTRACURRICULAR	Seminars, symposiums.
REFERENCES	Furnished upon request.

---

13. *Medical clerk/receptionist*

Education is listed first to draw attention to the fact that she is studying medical office management. The employment experience reflects her background in that field. Skill descriptions tie in capabilities related to medical office duties.

RESUME SAMPLE 13

JUDY JOB SEEKER — RESUME

333 Third Street
Jobsville, CA 33333 — Telephone (415) 333-3333
Messages (415) 233-1111

OBJECTIVE	Seeking a position as a clerk-receptionist, in medical or other

fields, with an established office offering career opportunity and growth.

EDUCATION ⇦

March present (evening)	1980–	Bryman School San Francisco, CA Medical office management
October January	1978– 1979	University of San Francisco San Francisco, CA Certificate: clerical skills training program
September June	1976– 1978	Woodrow Wilson High School San Francisco, CA General education

EMPLOYMENT EXPERIENCE

March June	1978– 1980	Roland's Soul City San Francisco, CA *Cashier* Responsible for making accurate cash reports and balancing statements, accurate record keeping, taking inventory, preparing petty cash for next cashier, purchasing supplies, managing store. Handled over $2,000 a day, worked under pressure, successfully met all deadlines.
June August	1978– 1978	San Francisco Municipal Railroad San Francisco, CA *Assistant Receptionist* Responsible for accurately typed letters, recommendations, complaints, interoffice hearings, as well as copying and retrieving personnel infor-

		mation. Developed and organized centralized filing system. Distributed incoming and outgoing mail, related well with irate riders and assisted in solving their problems.
June September	1977– 1977	Geneva Drive-In Theatre San Francisco, CA *Cashier*
		Made night drops, balanced tickets and sales, kept financial records and made daily cash reports. Handled up to $6,000 per night.
December December	1976– 1977	Kenneth Associates San Francisco, CA *Medical Billing Clerk*
		Responsible for typing medical insurance forms, accounts receivable, analyzing old records for past due payments, clarifying old billing statements, utilizing and understanding appropriate medical terminology, systematizing and updating old filing system, retrieving data from an IBM CRT computer terminal.
June September	1976– 1976	Young Community Development Company San Francisco, CA *Eligibility Investigator*
		Interviewed and investigated recipients of food supplements for eligibility.
REFERENCES		Furnished upon request.

14. *Architect*

Note "Summary of Skills"—used mainly with functional resumes.

RESUME SAMPLE 14

JUDY JOB SEEKER — RESUME

333 Third Street
Jobsville, CA 33333

Telephone (415) 333-3333
Messages (415) 233-1111

OBJECTIVE

Seeking to affiliate with an established firm offering advancement for measured achievement.

SUMMARY OF SKILLS

Successful in the following areas of architecture/design:

- Architecture
- Conceptual design
- Integration of interiors
- Custom furniture design
- Construction supervision
- Lighting
- Architectural materials/ finishes
- Budgeting/ installation
- Production staffing
- Drafting/ detailing

CAREER HIGHLIGHTS

Howard Hermanson & Associates
(a design corporation)
Portland, OR
Associate/Designer/Planner

Interior designer/architect for large-scale residential/commercial projects; associate-in-charge of ongoing renovation for Multnomah Athletic Club public areas.

John H. Thodos, Architect, P.C.
Portland, OR
Designer/Project Captain

Designer of small and medium-size residential/commercial project. Supervised production staff, coordinated work of associate engineers, supervised construction and performed administrative office supervision.

Skidmore, Owings and Merrill
(on loan)
Portland, OR
Designer

Developed preliminary design schemes for large-scale office, hotel and commercial projects.

Environmental Planning & Research
San Francisco, CA
Designer

Design, detailing and drafting of residence and commercial high-rise interiors. Also functioned as art director with responsibility of selecting all artwork for all commercial interior projects.

	Karl Treffinger and Associates San Francisco, CA *Designer*
	Design and site planning on hotels, associated commercial and recreational structures.
	Bassett, Horvath and Reiner San Francisco, CA *Designer/Draftsperson*
	Design, drafting and detailing on commercial interiors, commercial buildings and multihousing projects.
EDUCATION	
	Portland State University Portland, OR B.S. in social science; first- and second-year architecture, 1962
	University of Oregon Eugene, OR Third- and fourth-year architecture, 1963–1965
REFERENCES	Furnished upon request.

D. THE COVER LETTER

In Section Two—"Where and How to Look for a Job"—we will remind you again about the cover letter. Right now we are going to explain why it is necessary.

A cover letter is used when *anyone* asks you to send a resume and when replying to want ads by mail. Many do not respond to those types of want ads simply because they are not prepared. With a cover letter you will be prepared.

1. THE PURPOSES OF A COVER LETTER

a. It shows a certain level of *professionalism,* if nothing else. A typed one is best, but a handwritten one does the job.

b. It is another *sales tool.* We will demonstrate how that tool works in this section.

c. It is *competitive.* Doing it correctly gives you an advantage over your competition. Interviewers look forward to interviewing those who have sent in a professional presentation. Most often they open envelopes with nothing more in them than resumes—and not very good resumes!

d. It enables you to have a resume you can use for a number of jobs in a number of categories because the cover letter zeros in on the *particular* job and skills they request. Your resume may not, and so the cover letter is an aid to your resume.

People who have been through our program tell us that the interviewers praised their resume and cover letter. These job seekers could not even pass the application stage before using our methods, and now they were receiving numerous interviews and job *offers.* You must give the employers what they want to *see* and *hear* to win the job-seeking game, and the cover letter does just that. Even if you are marginally qualified, a cover letter will so impress the screeners so impressed with your presentation that you will be given an interview.

2. HOW TO COMPOSE A COVER LETTER

The cover letter should have three simple paragraphs to be effective:

a. *The opening*
Enclosed is my resume in reply to your position of ___________. (The wording can vary, but always keep it straightforward.)

b. *The body of the letter*

You will note from my resume that I (call attention to the skills you have that they list in their advertisement *first;* keep your statement *brief*).

c. *The closing*

I will look forward to talking with you regarding your position and my qualifications during the selection process.

That's it. Now *staple* it to your resume and send them in.

The first sample cover letter shows you how to reply, using a want ad as an example. Following that, there are several different cover letter samples for you to get the idea of how to do your own. If you do not get the idea, *get help.*

In Section Two we will tell you how to obtain a company's employment application form so that you can complete it and send it together with the resume and cover letter to make a complete Employment Package without running all over town to do it.

Our last words on cover letters are *do them.* Even if you do not type them and your handwriting requires a decoding expert, *do cover letters because they can do a lot for you!*

3. SAMPLE COVER LETTERS

Note the jobs for which the cover letters are written. Writing a cover letter will put you in a much stronger competitive position than that of other applicants who simply mail a copy of their resume.

Remember that the skills are "sold" in the second paragraph of the letter.

EXAMPLE OF A COVER LETTER ANSWERING A NEWSPAPER WANT AD WHERE A TELEPHONE CALL HAS BEEN MADE FIRST; NOTE THAT THE APPLICANT OBTAINED A COPY OF THE APPLICATION FOR EMPLOYMENT BEFORE REPLYING TO THE AD

Date

Nursery House
361 8th Street
San Francisco, CA 94102

Dear Ms. __________:

Enclosed is my resume and your completed application in reply to your advertisement in the *San Francisco Chronicle* for *general office help*. I appreciate your forwarding your application form so that I may present a complete presentation.

As you will note from my resume, I have general clerical and retail sales experience, am able to process sales orders with attention to detail and possess excellent written and telephone communication skills. I can file both alphabetically and numerically and am able to maintain excellent customer relations.

I will look forward to talking with you regarding the position and my qualifications during your selection process.

Sincerely,

Name

encls. 2

COVER LETTER OF AN INDIVIDUAL WITH NO HIGH SCHOOL DIPLOMA

Date

S.F. Automatic Fire Sprinkler Systems
981 South Carpret Street
San Bruno, CA 99999

Dear Sir:

I am enclosing my resume to apply for the position of *Apprentice Sprinkler Fitter.*

You will note from my resume that I have considerable technical/mechanical experience with a high mathematical aptitude and a genuine interest and desire to learn this trade.

I look forward to hearing from you so that we can talk in a personal interview.

Sincerely,

Name

encls.

COVER LETTER STRESSING KNOWLEDGE OF COMPLEX SYSTEMS

Date

American Micro Systems
87334 Old Home Road
Belmont, CA 94004

Dear Mr. Capar:

In response to our telephone conversation, I am sending you my resume for the position of *Clerk-Typist*.

I have two years' clerk-typist experience, type 35 wpm accurately, file alphabetically and numerically, can use business data systems and have handled heavy phone work taking and routing messages, using a 12-line Call Director.

I will look forward to talking with you regarding my qualifications and your position during your selection process.

Sincerely,

Name

encls.

COVER LETTER REPEATING LISTING OF "KEY" DUTIES TO UNDERSCORE MORE NUMEROUS DUTIES LISTED ON THE RESUME.

Date

Bullock's Personnel Department
135 Constitution Drive
Menlo Park, CA 94304

Dear Sir:

I am enclosing my resume in response to your advertisement for the position of *Shipping/Receiving Clerk.*

You will note from my resume that I have an extensive background in shipping/receiving, including such detailed duties as record-keeping, bills of lading, processing claims on damages and shortages, routing, comparison of quantities and order verification as well as use of equipment associated with shipping and receiving.

I will look forward to talking with you regarding my qualifications and your position during the selection process.

Sincerely,

Name

encls.

EXAMPLE OF "BRAGGING" IN A COVER LETTER TO DRAW IMMEDIATE ATTENTION TO PROFIT-STRUCTURE CONTRIBUTIONS; THE RESUME ELABORATES ON SUCCESSES

Date

Imperial Group Insurance
288 Sacramento Street
San Mateo, CA 94401

Dear __________:

Enclosed is my resume confirming our telephone conversation of this date.

As we discussed, I am interested in exploring sales career possibilities with your firm. I can bring a successful track record of over-quota sales, with the ability to follow established sales leads or create new customers by effectively establishing my own brand of cold-call leads. I am completely familiar with group insurance sales, having brought my former employer an account of 1,500 employees, resulting in a significant contribution to the profit structure of that firm.

I will look forward to talking with you further regarding your position and my qualifications.

Sincerely,

Name

encls.

THIS LETTER NOT ONLY LISTS ABILITIES BUT PERSONAL WORK TRAITS AS WELL

Date

Personnel Office
P.O. Box 4362
Brisbane, CA 94005

Dear Personnel Recruiter:

Enclosed is my resume for the advertised position of *Janitor.*

You will note, in my recent position with the County of San Mateo, that my responsibilities included: cleaning and waxing floors, shampooing and vacuuming carpets. I am able to operate hand power tools and am familiar with detergents, disinfectants and cleaning agents for special purposes and can perform minor carpentry and electrical repairs.

Other responsibilities were to keep the building exteriors, interiors and grounds neat and orderly. I pride myself in the ability to look up and down—not just straight ahead to perform tasks beyond what is required for minimum appearance.

I will look forward to talking with you during your selection process.

Sincerely,

Name

encls.

EXAMPLE OF A COVER LETTER STRESSING READINESS TO PRESENT SAMPLES OF THE APPLICANT'S ARTISTIC SKILLS

Date

Mr. Everett Fisher
American Graphics, Inc.
111 Second Street
San Francisco, CA 94411

Dear Mr. Fisher:

I have enclosed my resume listing my graphic arts background in commercial settings.

While my resume is specific in denoting my skills in various aspects of graphic arts, as well as my work history, I am prepared to make a portfolio presentation to you during your selection process so that you may see the high quality of my art.

I look forward to hearing from you soon.

Sincerely,

Name

encls.

E. THE INTERVIEW

1. WHAT IS AN INTERVIEW FROM THE EMPLOYER'S POINT OF VIEW?

An interview is granted when the employer deems you basically *qualified* (at least enough to call you in). They did not find anything alarming about your application or resume, so they want to see you to decide how comfortable you are with your skills and how comfortable they would be about having you work for their firm. (If they should make a poor choice, they would be responsible, of course.) They also need to hear your attitude about working for a living. But all the questions they ask you—some of them seemingly pointless, some not so pointless—boil down to these:

a. Will this person produce the work?
b. Will this person get along with others? ("Others" often means the department head as well as other employees.)
c. Does this person's attitude indicate that he or she will be promotable?

2. A WORD ABOUT DEPARTMENT HEADS TO BUSINESS AND INDUSTRY LEADERS

Of the thousands of actual participants and others exposed to our program, 27 percent did not understand the demands of business for profit or the role they needed to play to increase productivity. They are typical of those who can't find jobs and can't hold onto the jobs they do manage to find.

However, 60 percent of the remaining 73 percent who found jobs expressed personality conflicts with former supervisors. A certain number of the participants brought these conflicts on themselves, or did not know how to cope in the workplace. But a majority said they accepted their former jobs and were inspired to work and eager to produce and grow with the firm through their contributions. Once on the job, they found that their supervisor "held all the cards," whether the employee problem was justified or not. Frustrated, these workers were bewildered as to why a firm would allow tyrannical supervisors to force out employees because of the supervisors' petty insecurities. They could not understand why a firm did not recognize that this type of management supervision undermines the firm's productivity by driving away otherwise valuable employees.

Employers: There seems to be one such tyrant in many offices. In many ways, such firms are responsible for the poor market of job seekers about which they always complain. Don't think for a minute that your "grievance policy" is effective. Most people just walk away from the job, glad to be away from such mean, irrational supervisors. Worse yet, when these former employees attempt to obtain another job, the supervisor gives them only negative references. Even if you have a policy prohibiting information from being given, these vindictive supervisors suggest a bad reference by their negative tone of voice to the reference checker, and the former employee is again rejected. A portion of the new Department of Labor category of the unemployed, "too discouraged to look," can easily be attributed to this unfair and harmful use of supervisory authority. Take a good look at some of your supervisors and correct those who have demonstrated, by high department turnover, that they cannot get along with most of the people who report to them. Such an action might go a long way to increase productivity.

3. WHAT IS AN INTERVIEW FROM YOUR POINT OF VIEW?

"Oh, if I could only get the interview, I know I could get the job!" Remember saying that? Using our methods you will get interviews, and you will be halfway home to an offer if

you get one. Information on interviews in many other job-search books tell you (a) to be "positive" (without telling you what that means), (b) to sit up straight (very uncomfortable to most in a crisis setting), (c) to demonstrate your personality, (d) how to dress, (e) all the questions you are supposed to ask or not ask. All valuable advice. We will now go one step farther and give you *answers* to some of the basic "pressure" questions asked by interviewers. Before we do, you should know that many interviewers do not know the answers to those questions themselves. They ask them and determine your attitude and intentions from the way you respond. Thus, you screen yourself out.

At the start of the interview both you and the interviewer are nervous. *You* are about to face a total stranger who is in a position to extract from you personal information you would never tell even your best friend. The interviewer has to ask these questions.

However, you are *more* nervous than the interviewer. Even if you went to the rest room before the interview, you may have to go again. Your throat is dry the minute you sit down. In an effort to appear casual, you hang your arm over the back of the chair, scratch imaginary itches ever so delicately, cross and uncross your legs. Most interviewers excuse all of these things in the initial stages because they are sympathetic to your nervousness.

In our videotape library we have about 300 authentic interviews, in all vocational categories, of people of every age and educational level. The camera caught the stress of an actual interview. The amount of uncharacteristic body movements interviewers see is staggering. It's human nature, so nothing short of tying your hands behind you will correct it. Just be aware that these movements are reactions to stress and try to control them. One way is to fold your hands casually on your lap and dig one fingernail in the other palm, just short of drawing blood. The preferred way is to feel confident that you can field the questions that will be thrown at you.

4. TYPES OF INTERVIEWERS

Nice. They are mellow and they make you feel wanted and comfortable. They offer you coffee and chat about the company and the position until they feel you relax. Sympathetic to the stress of a job search, they want to do their job well and give every benefit to the individual they are interviewing because they *are* nice and they want the best person for the job. They enjoy their work and are very people-oriented. You think that if everyone is like them in the company, that's where you want to work. From the feedback we have received, there are too few of them. However, they will ask the same questions as someone who is . . .

Not nice. They are rigid, smug, no-nonsense, won't give an inch, are demanding and *tough.* They have taken every industrial relations course, seminar and workshop they can get to. They don't smile, lighten up for a second or give you any indication of how you stand, much less encouragement. A *department head* who interviews in this way will also supervise in the same manner if you are hired, so beware of the stern department head interviewer, since you have to work for him or her. But *you do not* have to work for the personnel person—you just have to get his or her approval and recommendation.

Sadists. They like to see you squirm. If you stumble on one devastating question, they will fire another at you while your nerve endings are still raw. The fact that they are allowed to make decisions about people makes them feel important, and they take every opportunity to exercise their power—at your expense. Your only defense is to walk out—in their midsentence, if necessary. *Why should you take that abuse?* You will reveal how uncomfortable you are and you won't be hired anyway, so you have nothing to lose. Keep your self-esteem by standing up, extending your hand and saying, "Excuse me for interrupting, but I don't like your style. I want to wish you all the luck in the world in filling your position." You walk out with your dignity undamaged, and they might learn something.

5. THE PANEL INTERVIEW

Usually three or more people interviewing at the same time comprise a panel. The members of the panel may either be related to the position for which they are hiring or they may have been asked to join the panel because of their individual expertise.

The panel interview creates pressures for the applicant, but there is really no way to get around it. All you can do is determine who is asking the pertinent and important questions, direct your answers at that person and merely glance at the rest and smile.

6. WHAT *NOT* TO DO IN AN INTERVIEW

a. *Do not rehearse an interview before you go.* If you are like most people, you try to create a script for the interview. ("Let's see, now; if they ask this, I'll say that.") But they never ask the questions exactly as you preworded them; therefore, you are completely thrown off your rehearsed answer. Often, the minute you walk in for the interview, you forget everything you prepared in the stark reality and panic of the moment.

b. *Don't go early.* Going early gives you too much time to feel disoriented, tense and like a stranger in an unfamiliar, unfriendly land. If the interviewer is late, both of you are nervous and annoyed. While you wait, you wonder why you are accepting the delay, but you invariably cop out when the interviewer finally enters and apologizes for making you wait. "Oh, that's all right!" It's not, of course, but that's what you say because you feel it's expected of you. Besides, you probably had just lighted a cigarette or spilled your cup of coffee.

c. *Don't smoke,* even if it is suggested. And don't ask if you may. It will be hard, particularly if they are smoking.

d. *Don't start reeling off all your personal problems.* You are there to sell your skills. Too many people, in interviews, start out with a positive answer to a question and then add unrelated material simply to pad the answer. A good interviewer will "bait" the person being interviewed by pretending interest, then let the person "hang" himself or herself. This is *not* a social encounter, no matter how comfortable you are; it is a *business* encounter. You are there to back up your application and resume and demonstrate that you are a pleasant person as well, *nothing more.* Remember, the interviewer's time is valuable. You are not the only one to be interviewed that day. Others are either waiting or are scheduled to be interviewed, and they are *your competition!*

e. *Don't knock your former supervisors' or former employers' methods.* It is always tempting to shift blame in a pressure situation. This is one of the worst things you can do in an interview and immediately makes you suspect. Even if they are still considering you, when they check references they will dig deep to find negative qualities about you if they feel you were overly defensive and shifted blame. There are two sides to every story, and they have heard only yours.

7. INTERVIEWER QUESTIONS: WHAT THEY MEAN AND HOW TO REPLY TO THEM

Understand the following questions but do not attempt to memorize all of them. Instead try to understand, from the employer's point of view, why the questions are asked. An interviewer will ask a question that may call for the same answer as one that has already been asked. Just try to realize that what they are getting at is *the profit structure of their firm and your role in that profit structure.* Tell them what they *want* to hear, for even if you do not, some of your competition will. When you understand how to react to questions in a way that meets the need of the employer, you will ace out your nearest competition, especially if you are equally qualified in demonstrating the right attitude and meeting employer expectations. DO NOT WORRY ABOUT *YOURSELF* UNTIL THE *OFFER*. WORRY ABOUT THEIR WELL-BEING AS A COMPANY THAT WILL PAY YOU MONEY TO PERFORM JOB DUTIES. WHEN THEY CALL YOU WITH AN OFFER THEY WANT *YOU*, AND THAT'S WHEN YOU NEGOTIATE WHAT IS BEST FOR YOU AS WELL AS FOR THEM.

The key to interviewing is to be a good listener and seize every opportunity to sell your skills, always emphasizing what your skills will do for the company. Instead of sitting there only half listening, terrified of what they may ask you next, LISTEN CAREFULLY AND TAKE YOUR CUE FROM WHAT THEY SAY OR ASK. TAKE ONE THING AT A TIME AND MAKE THE MOST OF EVERY CHANCE TO *BRAG*. IT'S THE ONLY TIME YOU CAN GET AWAY WITH BRAGGING. DURING A JOB SEARCH YOU ARE EXPECTED TO BRAG. DO NOT PULL THE MILD AND MEEK BIT DURING AN INTERVIEW. YOUR COMPETITION WON'T.

Key words are in italics in answers. The answers may seem corny to you, but not to interviewers.

QUESTION

What from your background, makes you a good candidate for this position?

Why they want to know

To see if you know your own skills and if you can tie them in to their needs.

ANSWER

"When I *quickly learn* your systems and methods, my skills will enable me to *handle* the work load *efficiently*."

QUESTION

Tell me something about yourself.

Why they want to know

Several reasons, among them (1) to allow you to trap yourself by introducing negatives; (2) to see how you see yourself.

ANSWER

"I *enjoy* working. It pleases me to know *a job is well done* and I have made a *contribution.* I am seeking a happy mix between my personal life and my vocational life." (THAT'S ENOUGH. WHO CARES IF YOU LIKE TO SEW? PLAY BASEBALL? SQUEEZE BEER CANS? ARE DIVORCED? HAD A HARD TIME IN LIFE? YOU ARE TALKING TO AN INTERVIEWER, NOT A PSYCHIATRIST! AND CERTAINLY NOT A FRIEND.)

QUESTION

What kind of position are you interested in?

Why they want to know

Unless you are applying for an advertised open position, they do not know. They are in the best position to have reviewed your application and resume and match your skills with the kind of jobs they hire for. However, choose several overlapping job titles that match your skills. If you are in a speciality area, name your speciality.

ANSWERS

"My speciality area is ________." "I see my skills in a number of positions with several titles. They are ______." How does that compare with the kind of jobs you have? (The game is back to them.)

QUESTION

Why do you want to work for us?

Why they want to know

They want to determine if you have researched their firm and if you know they are growing. Are you looking for a job or an *offer?* Do you now see the difference between a "job" and an "offer"? You should to make your job seeking effective.

ANSWERS

1. "*I have researched your firm and see you have a growth pattern. I want to use my skills and grow with the firm.*" Make sure you really have researched the firm if you give this answer! They may ask: "Oh, really? What kind of growth did you note, and where did you research us?" All mid-to-upper-management candidates must research a firm before being interviewed for that firm. Start your research at the library. If not, have the firm send you their annual report. They are loaded with positive information, so try to find out if there are any shortcomings in the company as well.
2. "*I am seeking a position that offers rewards for measured achievement. I want to make money and grow in the process. Does your firm offer these?*" Any firm that finds a person who wants to make money will realize that they will also make money for the company from their efforts to increase productivity.

"Why do you want to work for us?" is an unfair question. How would you know if you want to work for them or not? You have been there only 10 minutes. That's why, unless working for them has been a childhood dream, you must generalize about productivity, your skills and personal vocational growth. If they press further, tell them you have answered to the best of your ability.

QUESTION

What experience or training have you had that would strongly qualify you for this position?

Why they want to know

First of all, they already do know. They have your application and resume in front of them, and they would not have called you in for an interview unless you had either the appropriate experience or training. They want to see if *you* know. Just match your skills with their primary needs of productivity and profit. This goes for *everyone,* from entry level through upper management.

ANSWER

"Item ____ on my resume has given me the experience I need for this position." Pick one or two past jobs that most resemble what they will be asking you to do if they hire you. Zero in on *your* strongest skills for *their job.*

QUESTION

What are your strengths?

Why they want to know

This question determines your attitude toward work and your capabilities.

ANSWER

"Bringing all of my assignments to efficient and satisfactory conclusions." This is your cue to brag endlessly about your various skills as well as to make a statement about "getting along well with others."

QUESTION

What are your weaknesses?

Why they want to know

What will keep this person from doing a good job in their work. This question is a *trap.* Half of the applicants say, "I have no weaknesses"—a dumb answer. Everyone has weaknesses. The other applicants start listing negatives, primary among them an answer we have heard that other job-search programs recommend: "Sometimes I work too hard." Since "job burn-out" is a big corporate fear these days, don't give them cause to think you might become a victim of it. There is only one answer, and stick to it.

ANSWER

"*None that I would bring to the job.*" The ones not brought to the job are none of their business, but don't say it. No sense antagonizing the screener.

QUESTION

What are your salary requirements?

Why they want to know

We have already discussed that in the application section. If no salary has been quoted prior to the interview, this is where they determine if you're too high, too low or just right.

ANSWERS

1. "Negotiable." If no salary has been stated prior to the interview, this is the time to start playing the negotiating game once you receive an offer.
2. If they are advertising a flat salary (for example, $900 per month, $9.00 per hour, etc.), your answer is that the advertised salary is satisfactory to *start.*
3. If they have a stated salary range in their advertisement or job-opening notice, your answer is that salary is negotiable but "your salary range is within my requirements." Again, wait for the *offer* and then *negotiate!*

QUESTION

Did you have any problems with former supervisors or co-workers?

Why they want to know

They do not want their supervisors and workers to have to cope with your personality flaws if you are hired. Guilt often drives applicants in interviews to discuss their personality problems, thinking the company will find out anyway. If the company talks to former supervisors during a reference check *and* you have mended your bridges or have not listed the company in your application, you are O.K. If you have not, you could be in trouble.

ANSWER

Never answer "yes." A guilt trip about personality conflicts leads you to shift blame and makes them want to probe deeper. *You must straighten out any problems, following our advice, BEFORE you start job-hunting.* Remember, many supervisors must follow company policy and not give out that information. But smaller companies, especially "Mom and Pop" companies, freely give out negative references.

QUESTION

What would your references say about you if we called them?

ANSWER

"My references are in order." (They will be if you have done what we told you. At the very least, they will be rendered harmless.)

QUESTIONS

What did you like best about your last job? What least?

ANSWERS

Best: Name duties you know will be required in the job for which you are interviewing. This will give the interviewer an immediate "picture" of you doing their work.

Least: State *nothing* as far as the duties and the people were concerned. Poor equipment, the systems for work flow—these are harmless answers.

QUESTION

If we offered you a position, how long would you plan to stay?

Why they want to know

It costs money to train you in their systems, using and increasing your skills. You are an investment in time and money and, during that period, you are not 100 percent productive. This question is an attitude evaluator, a way of testing your maturity and sense of responsibility.

ANSWERS

The correct answer is that you "plan to stay" as long as there is "growth" opportunity *or* money rewards for your good work. This answer applies even if you are taking the job for survival.

If you are a student, earning money to go to school, you might state: "I expect to work for you as long as I am in school because I must work in order to go to school. After graduation, I would like to use the knowledge I gained in school here, but I would first want to review with you whether there is growth potential for me in this firm." Sure, it sounds corny, but it is to their advantage that you produce while learning and use that learning to produce more after graduation.

QUESTIONS

What are your goals in five years? In 10 years?

Why they want to know

They want to see if you have goals. They want to determine if you have false expectations of your own capabilities or if they can meet your growth expectations before they invest in you as an employee.

ANSWERS Same for both the five- and 10-year goals.

If you have such goals and they are realistic, tell them.

If you do not, tell them this: "I want to join a firm that

offers growth potential. I will have a chance to look around, once hired, to see where I would make the best contribution as I grow, and you will have a chance to evaluate me as well."

QUESTION

Why did you leave your last job?

ANSWER

It is on your application. Give the interviewer exactly the same information.

QUESTION

Do you plan future schooling?

ANSWER

"Yes, relative to my work. If I need to take courses that will improve my growth opportunities with the firm from which I accept an offer, I am willing to do this." (Most companies will pay the tuition of such courses if they are related to their firm's needs and if you pass the course. In some cases, they will send you to courses.)

QUESTION

Why should we hire you? The toughest question in interviewing. It produces instant stress.

ANSWER

The most common reply given to this question is, "Because I am qualified for the job." Don't use it. So are all of the other applicants, and you don't know if you are more qualified than they are. *There is only one answer:*

"Because my *skills* and *efficiency* will contribute to your *profit structure.*" (All they care about, at this point, is you in relation to their profits. If you are interviewing for a bureaucratic job, "profit" becomes "goals and philosophies." The words change, but the basic answer is the same.)

QUESTION

Are you single, married, divorced?

Why they want to know

To see how comfortable you are with who you are. It is easy to react emotionally to this question; that is what they expect. Do not. Simply state, "I am ________." *No elaboration, no stories, no woes.*

QUESTION

Who will take care of your children while you work?

Why they want to know

Time away from work is nonproductive. Time is money to business.

ANSWER

"My children are provided for so I can work (full time/part-time)." It is not necessary to tell them how.

QUESTION

What transportation do you have to get to and from work?

ANSWER

"I have reliable transportation." Even if you do not at the time, you can make arrangements later if you get an offer.

QUESTION

Do you have any questions for us?

Why they want to know

Other job-search books suggest "appropriate" questions to ask, but we recommend against doing this. Since this question comes toward the end of the interview, you could spoil the positive atmosphere already established. Asking questions simply because you think you are "supposed" to can demonstrate a negative attitude—if they are the wrong questions. These questions should come when they make you an *offer* and are harmless at that point.

ANSWER

"Not at this time."

This indicates that you expect to be called back for another interview or *made an offer.* It is a positive statement that indicates that their description was complete and that *you know when to ask questions.* Don't detract from your presentation or waste their time. And don't make the mistake of trying to clinch the interview by asking the screener to take the time to read your glowing references. That's another waste of their time. The interviewer feels "obligated" to read them and comment. Have you ever read a *bad* letter of reference? Letters of reference are merely good protection against a bad verbal reference from someone who forgot they gave you a good reference in writing! If you feel you must use them, have them copied in sets and present a set to the interviewer in this manner: "By the way, here is a set of my reference letters to add to my Employment Package." That way you do not waste their time, while you sit there, obligating them to read your references there and then. If they are considering you, they will read them afterward. It's less awkward for you and them when you're not there at the time they read them.

8. LAST WORDS ABOUT INTERVIEWS

These questions may be asked in a somewhat different form than given here but are easily identifiable in any form. Have you noted how your responses will be interpreted as either harmless or directed to the ultimate "good of the company"? We hope so. When you get the *offer,* you can worry about your own well-being. And if you do not like *their* answers, *don't accept the offer.* Remember, we're teaching you to go after *more than one offer.* Word all your answers to enhance the good of the firm. Use your own words, but make them mean the same as we have stated them here. Enter that interview determined to tell them what you can do for *them,* and *sell your skills.* Never get too comfortable in an interview. Always be on guard against questions that may encourage you to reveal too much about yourself. Just stick to what you wrote on your application and resume.

You do not have to be a movie star, oozing personality from every pore, lighting up the room with your glow. Just come across as a person who is serious about contributing to productivity and profits and who will "grow" in the process and create vocational forward momentum for yourself.

If the interviewer keeps glancing down or over at the same spot when you are talking, beware—it may be one of those infernal "voice stress machines." They have been marketed to companies as a "hiring aid." Supposedly this little machine will reveal undue or abnormal stress in your answers to certain questions the interviewer asks. There is no protection against these electronic spies. But who would want to work for a company that uses them? Lie-detector tests (these may be used for jobs requiring security clearances) and handwriting analysis are examples of other devices used to "help" an interviewer evaluate an applicant.

Whatever happened to hiring someone because the interviewer trusted his or her instincts?

F. THE THANK-YOU LETTER

1. HOW TO WRITE A THANK-YOU LETTER

There is one more item to add to your application, resume, professional cover letter and interview to create a perfect Employment Package presentation: *You have to write a thank-you letter for the interview.* It is the ultimate "weapon" in destroying your competition. It can be merely a routine note, or it can be used to "repair" any point that might have damaged you in the interview. *Sending a thank-you letter is a professional courtesy and has unlimited impact on hiring for decision makers!* Like the cover letter, it usually has three paragraphs; sometimes an extra paragraph will be needed to emphasize a point or stress your qualifications.

1. I want to take this opportunity to thank you for the time you spent with me on______, regarding your position for _____________.
2. After talking with you, I am convinced that my skills in ________(*list them, starting with the most important* to their job opening) can be quickly transferred to your systems and methods so that I can make an immediate contribution. (Now, if you noticed any questionable reaction to something you said in regard to your being able to perform the work, you can repair it in the last sentence of this paragraph.)
3. I look forward to hearing from you soon.

Read the following sample thank-you letters. If you mishandled something in the interview, revert back to a statement in the thank-you letter that demonstrates your understanding of the world of work: Efficiency + skills = productivity and profit. You can find the wording to use in these sample letters.

2. SAMPLE THANK-YOU LETTERS

1. Date

Mrs.________
Personnel Department
Nicolet Technology Corporation
145 East Dana Street
Mountain View, CA 94041

Dear Mrs.________:

I want to take this opportunity to thank you for the time you spent interviewing me, as well as for the time the supervisor spent with me on Tuesday, March 3, regarding the Electromechanical Assembly position.

As I mentioned to you, I do have considerable experience in electromechanical assembly, and as I told the supervisor, I am looking for job growth potential.

I look forward to hearing from you and thank you again for your time.

Sincerely,

Name

2. Date

Mr.________,
Service Manager
Engineered Communication and Service
3350 Victor Court
Santa Clara, CA 95050

Dear Mr.________:

I want to take this opportunity to thank you for the time you spent interviewing me, as well as the time the supervisor spent with me on April 2, regarding the Sound Technician/Service Installer position.

As I mentioned to you, I have experience in the installation of sound and alarm systems, both large and small. I do troubleshooting and repair of systems as well. It appeared to me that your company offers the growth potential for measured achievement that I am looking for, and this is the type of work I want to be doing.

Thank you again for your time.

Sincerely,

Name

3. Date

Mr.________, Superintendent
Holy Cross Cemetery
Mission Road
Colma, CA 94013

Dear Mr.________:

I would like to thank you for going over my work application and resume with me last Wednesday.

I was very impressed with Holy Cross Cemetery and feel that it is the kind of place where I would like to work. The work I did for Cabrillo School District has prepared me to work in a groundskeeping setting and with the equipment required. You will find me conscientious, hardworking and willing and able to learn quickly any task that will make me a better worker.

Looking forward to hearing from you favorably, I am,

Yours truly,

Name

4. Date

Mrs.________
Potlatch Corporation
P.O. Box 3591
San Francisco, CA 94119

Dear Mrs.________:

I want to take this opportunity to thank you for talking with me on Tuesday regarding the Receptionist position. I also appreciated talking with Mrs.________about the position and the growth potential of the company.

As we discussed, I am familiar with practically every procedure you related, including the use of the rotary line phone system. That, coupled with my clerical abilities and sequential skills, would make me an ideal candidate for the position, and I know I can make a valuable contribution to the profit structure of the Potlatch Corporation.

I look forward to receiving an offer for this position.

Yours truly,

Name

5. AN ADDITIONAL PARAGRAPH IS USED STRESSING THE APPLICANT'S EXPERIENCE THAT WOULD BE EFFECTIVE FOR A JOB IN A CONVALESCENT HOSPITAL

Date

Ms.________
Director of Personnel
St. Mary Convalescent Pavilion
93 Pardonna Street
Daly City, CA 94015

Dear Ms.________:

Thank you for taking the time to talk with me on Monday regarding your Receptionist position.

My professional background has prepared me to use the telephone as a business tool, take and route calls with efficiency, direct visitors and clients to the proper source of inquiry within the company and accept routine clerical tasks. I understand the humanistic nature of your business, and I feel that I can contribute that something extra by making myself available when needed beyond the job duties.

I am able to work alone or as part of a team and am expressly interested in your position because I possess the sensitivity as well as the skills you seek.

I will look forward to discussing your position and my qualifications with you again and with the staff members with whom I would interact.

Sincerely,

Name

6. AN ADDITIONAL PARAGRAPH IS USED TO PUNCH HOME THE APPLICANT'S INTEREST IN GROWTH POTENTIAL

Date

Mr.________
Personnel Office
Homequity
2600 Campus Drive
San Mateo, CA 94403

Dear Mr.________:

I would like to thank you and Mrs.________for the time you spent with me on the 26th regarding the Mail Clerk position. I found our meeting both enjoyable and informative.

As mail clerk for Homequity, I can bring not only the ability to perform as an efficient, energetic clerk, but can also contribute various other office skills to assist in any way I can in the obviously smooth functioning of your work force.

Not lost on me was the fact that the position can lead to advancement within the company, thereby encouraging growth potential on my part.

I will look forward to hearing from you again.

Sincerely,

Name

7. MORE THAN ONE PARAGRAPH TO EMPHASIZE THE APPLICANT'S SKILLS

Date

Mr.________
Margruder Plastics
123 B Street
San Jose, CA 93654

Dear Mr.________:

I want to thank you for talking with me regarding the Driver/Shipping-Receiving position with your firm.

I possess excellent manual dexterity, have an excellent driving record, am well aware of safety procedures, am strong, can pull stock and perform inventory and have a knowledge of shipping/receiving procedures and related manual and power machines.

I am particularly interested in associating with a growing company, such as you stated yours is, to take advantage of growth potential through measured achievement.

I hope to hear from you soon.

Sincerely,

Name

Now you are ready for the actual job search. You have the following means to create an Employment Package:

a. How to write a cover letter.
b. How to complete an application for employment, in detail, designed to "dazzle" a screener.
c. How to write a resume as a skills sales tool.
d. How to answer interview questions.
e. How to write a thank-you letter.

Make sure you understand how to handle all of the above before you go on to Section Two: "How and Where to Look for a Job." *Get help* if any of the items above are unclear!

SECTION TWO

WHERE AND HOW TO LOOK FOR A JOB

A. TAKING THE FIRST STEP

Write a sentence describing your skills. To learn how to do this, review the second paragraph of the cover letter samples. If one sentence seems too long, break down the description of your skills into two sentences. Start with your strongest skills first, then the lesser (but just as important) ones and add a statement about "working well with others."

Now staple or clip your master application, resume and sentence together and set them aside. You will need *all three* for what we are about to teach you.

B. THE MOST COMMONLY KNOWN WAYS TO LOOK FOR A JOB

They are listed below *not* in the order of their importance. We will teach you what you need to know about each one.

1. The walk-in
2. Employment agencies
3. The unemployment office
4. Civil service
5. Friends and business associates
6. Want ads/
   The telephone

Emphasis will be placed on want ads and the telephone. But let's begin at the beginning.

1. THE WALK-IN

Some job seekers will walk in *cold* to a company and say something that amounts to: "HI, GOT ANY JOBS?" *Except* for service/construction trades, this is the *worst* way to look for a job. But at least you will be armed with a resume and a master guideline for preparing their application in a detailed manner—on the spot, if necessary. Proper use of the telephone, however, will enable you to avoid running madly about, crashing unannounced into personnel offices and facing awkward situations.

2. EMPLOYMENT AGENCIES

People do not know how to approach employment agencies properly, much less use them properly. Employment agencies are in business to make money. Because some of them have bad reputations, they are used by a good many people as a last resort. If you are obligated to pay the agency fee, they will *want their money as soon as they refer you to a job and you are hired.* Naturally, you have been unemployed and may have no money, so they work out a payment-of-fee schedule that may involve interest payments on top of the fee. Your first reaction, after being hired as a result of their involvement, is relief at having a job, but agencies have experienced many no-pay situations. At first, you plead with them for a job. But after you get one from them, you cry to everyone how expensive it was. Some people ignore the fee involved for the agency referral and end up having their salary attached at the new job.

One way to avoid this is to go to one or more of the agencies where the fee is paid by the employer. These agencies will have a 30-day cash flow for their efforts on your behalf. They refer you, you get the job, the employer pays them in 30 days.

Approach employment agencies as we have taught you to approach an *employer.* They will have you complete an employment application and then interview you to see how well and how fast they can "sell" you to an employer.

Receipt of their money depends on how well and how fast they do it. But how many times have you been to an agency (as a last resort) without receiving help from them? The main reason was because they evaluated you negatively as a desirable applicant. If they referred you to a company and you were not appropriate in terms of skills or attitude, this would reflect on their credibility with that employer. Their repeat business would suffer. Therefore, when you go to an employment agency, complete their application as you would an actual employer's form (remember the importance of detail), then interview with them as if they were going to *hire* you. They may even ask the same questions a screening interviewer would. It is their only way of measuring your attitude toward working, as well as determining and matching your skills. Knowing what you now know, you should easily impress them enough to refer you.

Don't be discouraged if they do not have an immediate in-house job order that fits your skills. If you impress them, they will try to locate a job opening, either with an established employer account or a new account. These people are professionals who, if effective, make good money. Not only do they advertise their services to clients, they advertise to firms as well. They do not wait for jobs to come to them; they actively go after openings with companies. (Later we are going to teach you how to find job openings that are *not* advertised. These are in the "hidden job market." It requires the simple use of the telephone—much as successful employment agencies use it, but in a slightly different and infinitely more clever way. The agency people are experts with the telephone, and you can be too.) There is no harm in registering yourself with several agencies. May the best agency win! Agencies where the employer pays the entire fee are advertised in the Yellow Pages and the want ads. While you are conducting your own job search, keep in touch with them once a week, even if you have not heard from them. Tell them you are "checking in." If, at the end of three weeks, they have produced no referral results, try another agency.

3. THE UNEMPLOYMENT OFFICE

Every town has one. They call it the Employment Office. We call it the Unemployment Office, because the only time anyone goes there is when they are *un*employed. They list jobs on a board or, depending on their efficiency and their budget, on microfiche, which at least is fun to use. Some local offices are very good; others are *not.*

The number of employers cooperating with them by listing their job openings is entirely dependent on the reputation of those government offices in the local business community. If they have their act together, refer appropriately and efficiently administer the job openings, the volume will be higher. Some even run job-search workshops. Look into them, but remember that the people running them are basically government employees with little or no business experience. For all their good intentions, they are still in the human services field, not in business for profit. They will counsel you, and some job counselors will refer you to a job developer. That means that person will *get* a job for you. Some need this type of help, most do not. Besides, there is the *dependency* factor. You go into a job that has been *"gotten"* for you and, from the beginning, the employer is skeptical of you because someone had to *do* this *for* you. If something happens to that job and you are no longer eligible for a social program, how do you help yourself?

Employment Office people use the *Dictionary of Occupational Titles* to locate your vocational classification. If they can't find it exactly, they come as close as they can.

Unfortunately, the Employment Office staff sometimes sends people to listed job openings long after the job has been filled. You are handed a referral card, sent on your way on a bus, and arrive only to find that the job has been filled for three weeks!

However, they do have job listings—good ones and weird ones. When they refer you to one, *ask them to phone for an appointment for you. It is a mistake to pursue that referral until they do!* The idea here is not to waste your time.

4. CIVIL SERVICE

Some people want to work in government service for the "human services" aspect, some for the benefits and some for the "security." Lately, you can strike that last reason because of human services budget cuts and government hiring freezes. When you locate an opening (at city, county, state or federal personnel offices), take the test and then immediately look for another job. If you pass the test, you will be put on a list. But you should be forewarned: many of these jobs are very much in demand, and the lists are long. So, even though you have passed the test, don't just sit by the phone and wait to be called. You should continue to look for a job. If necessary, take a job while you are waiting. If your name then reaches the top of the list, you can resign and accept the civil service job—if you still want it.

5. FRIENDS AND BUSINESS ASSOCIATES

If you are referred by a friend or business associate, you better back up their faith in you by referring you. If you get the job and "blow" it, it reflects not only on you but on them as well. You might lose a friend or business associate if you do not act professionally, either when applying or leaving, if after being hired you decide you don't want to stay. (See "How to Change Jobs" section.)

Now that you know what you need to know to use ways 1 through 5 effectively to locate job openings, you are ready for the two most generally effective methods. Let the others work for you, but *concentrate* on the next two methods.

6. WANT ADS

The "experts" say that the want ads are the least effective means to find work. They say this because most people do not know how to use want ads effectively, no matter what their educational level. Searching want ads for openings for *your* skills is frustrating, mainly because of the thousands of job titles that now exist. A janitor is also called "maintenance engineer"; 20 years ago, an administrative assistant meant something entirely different than it does now.

Many people get discouraged with want ads because the ads list *some* of the skills they have, then list others they *do not* have. To answer or not to answer? Answer if the skills listed *first in the ad* match yours. Whether or not you are accepted for an interview pretty much depends on the manner in which you apply. Some companies only hope to find individuals with the less important skills; some require them but would overlook your not having these if you indicate you have the more important skills. A smart company will list the most needed skills first in their ads and the "hope to find" skills last.

They will always be willing to see you if you have the important skills, *particularly if you use the "dazzle" factor we teach you in this book.* How can they turn down that kind of presentation? If you have the important skills, do not let lack of "trailing" skills keep you from applying. If you come across as "sharp," they will know you are capable of quickly learning the lesser requirements. If you apply and you do not hear from them, you will know the later-listed skills in the want ad were more important after all. But, as the saying goes, you don't know until you try! Don't assume. Apply anyway. Keep your options *open.*

a. Types of want ads and how to apply

The "el cheapo" ad. One or two uninspiring lines. *Clerk-typist, full-time. Call 574-7644.* "Must be a lousy place and job," you say? Maybe. But you don't know until you find out, do you? Again, do not assume. It could be and probably is a small company. But, then again, the company could have just the working atmosphere you prefer, with growth potential. Go for the *offer* and either *turn it down* or *negotiate,* if low salary is the problem. You now know how! Once you are hired, if you don't like the job or the management after a reasonable period of time—say, two or three months—reread the section on "How to Change Jobs," which appears later in this book.

The medium-to-large ad and the display ad. Concentrate on the phrases—skills desired/required/preferred. Pay attention to anything labelled "must" *and* the instructions for applying. There are two ways they ask you to apply:

b. *Responding to specific ads by telephone*

At the end of the ad, it will say something like (a) call Personnel, 574-7644, (b) call Barbara, 574-7644 or (c) call 574-7644.

If a person's name is listed, he or she may or may not be in Personnel. A large company could use the "personal" approach and place the personnel screener's name in the ad, or that person could just be someone set up in the firm to screen the calls they receive. It makes no difference; your approach will be the same. If the ad simply says, "call 574-7644," do so and say: "I would like to speak to the person handling the want ad________." Then *wait!*

When you speak with the person handling the want ad, here is what to say—*nothing more:*

A. "MY NAME IS________."
B. READ YOUR SKILLS SENTENCE LISTING *YOUR* SKILLS FIRST THAT MATCH THE SKILLS *THEY LIST FIRST* IN THE AD.
C. "WHEN MAY I COME FOR AN INTERVIEW?"

DO NOT ALLOW THE PERSON ON THE OTHER END TO SAY *ONE WORD UNTIL* YOU HAVE FINISHED—*STRAIGHT THROUGH.* YOU HAVE ASKED A QUESTION THAT MUST BE *ANSWERED.* YOU HAVE ALSO IDENTIFIED YOUR SKILLS FOR THE POSITION. If they ask screening questions over the phone, you have your master application and resume in front of you to relate back details on what they ask. You are *prepared!* Prepare the necessary information for the job and just keep going.

Imagine what these people are used to hearing. Both from personal experience and reports and complaints from people who handle want-ad calls, the usual response they get runs like this: "Hello, I'm calling about the ad. How much does the job pay? What are the benefits? I can work every day but Wednesday afternoon. Is that O.K.? Is there a bus to the door? When would I be reviewed for my first increase?"

Everything they ask is for *their* benefit, but they do not express any interest in what they can do for the *company.* Inasmuch as want ads with telephone numbers are fair game for anyone, you have to pity the poor devil handling the calls. Then *you* call. You identify yourself, state your business, sell your skills and ask for an interview. That is all they want to hear. They can't see you, so what else would they *want* to hear at that point?

Surprisingly enough, many times, even after you have done all this, they will say: "You will have to come in and fill out an application," or "Send us a resume." Why did they put their phone number in the paper if that's what they want? It is an unsolved mystery. However, more times than not, you will get an interview appointment based on your presentation. Even if they say "application" or "resume," that's fine, too—it gives you a chance to show your stuff with a cover letter and resume. Tell them: 'I am very busy with interviews right now. Could you *mail* me your application? I will return it with my *resume.*' They will 95 percent of the time because of your presentation, and now you have let them know you have a resume. That will impress them. You do not have to run all over town to fill out an application with no guarantee of an interview. You can make an effective "unseen" presentation from *home.*

If they *will not* mail you an application, ask them, "If I come in, will I receive an interview at that time?" If they say "No," decide if you want to go in. If they are courteous and apologetic about not mailing one, go in. If not, don't bother; you probably would not enjoy working for them anyway.

c. *The Telephone Method for Tapping the Hidden Job Market*

The employment agencies are trying to slot you in. You have visited the Employment Development Department. You have tapped friends and business associates and are waiting for the edition of the newspaper with the most want ads. There's one more thing you can do that has proved to be more effective than all of them: Use the telephone. Why? Because only 28 percent of the job market is *visible.* Most of it is below the surface. We are going to give you a method to uncover those job openings by a brazen, clever use of the telephone. It is also a way of obtaining interviews without first submitting an application or resume.

By using the telephone effectively, you can canvass the companies likely to use you in their business. If nothing is available in your most desired categories, you can try at another job level until something becomes available in the field you want. This is how to *survive* instead of feeling sorry for yourself and telling your friends "There is simply *nothing* available out there!"

If you think using the telephone requires great skill, you're wrong. A special class of 15 inner-city black youth aged 15 to 18 late on a Friday afternoon (traditionally the worst time of the week to look for a job) "practiced" for the first time the approach we are about to give you. These kids uncovered 51 job openings using the "cold call" method *in 45 minutes!* We were stunned! And they were not menial jobs—they were positions paying $600 to $1,000 per month. After the first three calls, these kids were winners!

Why were they successful? (and the answers apply to you, too!)

1. In "cold calling" they were any person they wanted to be on the phone.
2. They were armed with the same tools to make an effective presentation you now have, too.

3. They understood that *not* finding a job opening on every call did not mean rejection. Instead, they saw themselves as conducting a canvassing operation to locate unadvertised job openings and did not look on the exercise as a test of their popularity or self-worth.

Why it works on several fronts: The employers may need help, may be expanding, or may want to get rid of dead wood but do not have the time to find a replacement for a person barely doing his or her job. Your "cold call" may be more welcome than you think. It could solve the employer's personnel problem without any real effort on his part.

What to do if you get in trouble during the call. If you are directly challenged during the call, hang up! They don't know who you are. Just have a laugh on yourself because you "blew" it, and get on with the next call.

Before you make that first call:

1. You will need your skills sentence or sentences, your master application and your resume in front of you.

2. Call companies *likely* to hire someone having your skills. Some of you have skills that most companies use. Firms using clerks, bookkeepers, receptionists and restaurant and fast-food workers have many categories of jobs, *and many of these firms will train you.* Construction companies, property management firms and those hiring people in related blue-collar trades are listed in the Yellow Pages. Use the Yellow Pages index to determine the appropriate classification of skill. Larger business firms with both entry-level and more sophisticated positions in your area are listed with the local Chamber of Commerce. Many Chambers of Commerce publish a listing of local firms, and there are always library reference sources.

3. Make a list of the names and phone numbers of ten companies that you know hire people with your skills or might do so. Keep your list so you don't duplicate calls.

Once you're on the phone. You need the cooperation of the person answering the telephone. When anyone answers, you say: "Hello, I am *supposed* to talk with the person in charge of (the name of your skill). Would you tell me the person's name, please?"

You are now professionally appealing to their knowledge of the company, their courtesy and the reason they are allowed to answer the telephone.

If the person taking the call asks "What is this in reference to?" *repeat* "I am supposed to talk with the person," etc. "Can you help me or transfer me to a person who can?"

That person may refer you to Personnel if the company is large. Repeat the same question to the person in Personnel. A company large enough to have a Personnel Department may have more than one person "in charge" or more than one department handling hiring those with your skill. Personnel will *tell* you this. They may mention a name. "That's it," you should say. "Can you transfer me, or should I call back?" You now have a name. Write it down and ask them to spell it, if necessary. Even if they are wrong, when you speak to the person they mentioned, he or she will probably know exactly whom you should talk with. And then you have *another* name.

Now you will deal with receptionists and secretaries, unless you are lucky and the person you want answers the call, which can happen more often than might be expected. If you get the secretary, ask for the person whose name you have. "May I tell her (or him) who is calling?" is the kind of response you'll get. Give your name. Don't give your first name; just identify yourself as: Mr.______ or Mrs.______ or Ms.______.

If the person asks, "May I tell her (or him) what this call is in reference to? Just answer, "I am *supposed* to talk with so-and-so," etc. Be courteous.

If the person is not in, find out when he or she will return, and record the name at that time. In that way, you will not miss any names in your canvassing.

If they do not have an opening appropriate for you, they will say so. Then you say, *"Do you expect any in the near future?"* Your call may start them thinking about the people barely doing their job in your skills category and they may ask you to call back.

If they ask you who told you that they may have an opening, pick a name out of the air. Because an associate or friend of an associate may have referred someone to them, they will not question this. If they can't identify the person you named, tell them it is a friend of a friend. If it gets too awkward, repeat, "Do you have an opening?" If it gets impossible to continue the conversation, hang up!

Sometimes you cannot avoid Personnel. Should that be the case, read them your skill sentence and ask if they have openings. *Call Personnel direct, if you know the company is very large, to avoid being shunted from department to department.* This approach works. You might make 50 calls before you find an opening, or you might find one on the fifth call. But you are canvassing the hidden job market, and if you wait for notice of a job opening in a newspaper, you are your own worst enemy. Make five to 10 calls a day and you will find a job opening within a short period of time. You know what to do after you find the opening. This kind of job-hunting can be kind of fun when you know you can just hang up if you get into trouble! Some of the reactions to your calls will floor you.

Rarely will you have competition for the jobs you uncover. If you do, you will be miles ahead of them because of your professional presentation and the initiative you showed in making the call.

Just to humor you, some of the answerers may ask you to send a resume. Do so *only if there is an actual job opening.* Soon you will be able to tell the difference between genuine interest and a soft brushoff. Don't waste time sending resumes unless you sense genuine interest.

d. By mail

This is more frustrating because it is not as immediate as calling in response to a want ad. Be very careful with this type of want ad. There is a wait involved. They are collecting applicants unseen, and are not in the hurry that *you* are. They will have from one to two or three instructions that must be followed. What we said about the application form—if you can't follow instructions on an application, you can't follow instructions on the job—applies here too.

They may ask you for one or all of the following:

Resume

Salary history

Salary requirements (or minimum salary requirements)

The following want-ad examples and their explanations are the best way to demonstrate how to respond to them. See want-ad example 4 for dealing with salary history. See want-ad example 7 for dealing with minimum salary requirements.

Any other statement about salary requirements in a cover letter should be in a single paragraph before your last paragraph and should simply state, *"Of course, salary is negotiable."* Use this phrase when they ask for just plain "salary requirements."

It is always a good idea to make photocopies of your cover letters and staple the want ad to it, so you can keep track of to whom you sent what for each job. If you have followed our advice in this book, the offers will start to come in *immediately.* If you have five interviews with no results, you are doing something wrong. Try to trace back to uncover mistakes. Realistically look at your skills and see if they match the job you are seeking.

e. *Sample Want Ads: How to Interpret and Answer Them*

THESE WANT ADS ARE SANE AND SENSIBLE. YOU WILL ALSO RUN INTO SOME VERY KOOKY WANT ADS. DON'T LET THEM GET YOU DOWN—YOU WILL LEARN QUICKLY HOW TO IDENTIFY THEM. JUST THINK OF THEM AS "GOOD PRACTICE."

OFFICE CLERK—Staffing coordinator. Nurses Registry. Heavy phone work and PR. Call 237-9809. betwn. 9 and 3.

What does it tell you?

a. The only skills required (at least as far as mentioned in the ad) are phone work and public relations, which means you have to be able to handle the phone as a professional tool, plus have some savvy with people.

b. It is a *service* firm. The people calling the company want nurses.

c. They are prepared to take your call during certain hours listed.

Your approach

Step 1. Call between 9 and 3, ask for the person handling the want ad.

Step 2. State your name and read your skill sentence, emphasizing ability to handle the telephone as a "professional sales/public-relations" tool, as well as professionally "handling" people. End with, "When may I come for an interview?"
If they ask for a resume, ask them to send you an application to return completed, with the resume. (Complete your package with a cover letter!)

Step 3. If you have to forward a resume that does not mention heavy phone work, tell them in your cover letter, second paragraph, that you handled heavy phone work as well in your jobs.

> Counter person/cleaners FT. Will train. Salary open. Send resume to Ad #1234 this paper.

What does it tell you?

a. No experience necessary. They will *train.*
b. Salary is negotiable. Play the negotiating game. Get them to make an offer.
c. You have no idea where it is located, not even a phone number to give you a clue.
d. Nothing about the duties; therefore you must use *logic* when you write the cover letter (see below).

Your approach

Visualize what happens when you take in your cleaning and write a cover letter like the following, using logic.

Ad #1234
Daily Blatt
Gotham, U.S.A. (Zip Code)

Enclosed is my resume in reply to your ad for the position of *Counter Person.*

I have an excellent attitude with people to insure repeat business, am very detailed in my work, mature and enjoy customer service.

I will look forward to talking with you in a personal interview.

Very truly yours,

Mail it with your resume and continue your job search.

> DELIVERY, full- or part-time, male or fem., to deliver light boxes to businesses. 234-1234 betwn. 12 and 4 PM.

What does it tell you?

a. You have to have a driver's license. Because of their insurance premiums you must have a good driving record. (In California, more than two moving violations in the past three years can eliminate you.) Go to your local Department of Motor Vehicles, pay them $.50 to $1.00 and they will telex for a copy of your record while you wait. Make copies and take them with you to the interview, or mail one with your resume and application. (The firm will not pay "assigned risk" premiums just to hire you if your driving record is poor.)

b. A male or female is acceptable for the job.

c. No heavy lifting (light boxes).

Your approach

Step 1. Call them between 12 and 4 P.M. (*not* 11:30 or 4:30). Ask for the person handling the want ad for Delivery.

Step 2. When that person is on the line, start with "My name is________." (Read the skill sentence if you have driving/delivery experience or anything remotely connected with driving/delivery. If not, use logic.) "I have an excellent driving record and can furnish you with a copy of it. I am aware of the importance of safe driving practices and the need for prompt delivery. When may I come for an interview?" (If they want a resume, ask them to send you an application to return with your resume.)

CLERK-SECRETARY

Due to a recent promotion, we have an immediate need for an experienced Clerk/Secretary to support three people in our regional sales office.

Duties will consist of typing letters and quotations, filing, use of TWX/TLX and extensive phone work. Requirements include accurate typing (50 wpm), an excellent phone manner, willingness and ability to work unsupervised. Previous work experience in a sales/marketing department with word processing and dictating machine would be an asset.

For consideration, send your resume and salary history to BAC Co., 2700 Mayloo Lane, Suite 120, Middletown, U.S.A. 94362. [213] 549-1110. Resume and salary history will be accepted by mail only. An equal-opportunity employer M/F/H.

What does it tell you?

a. They know what they want.

b. Heavy work load—heavy typing/phones/assignments. Probably good pay if you are expected to support three people.

c. They *require* 50 wpm typing and will ask you to prove it with a test.

d. Sales/marketing background, word processing and dictating-machine people are your competition. Notice this is an "asset," but lack of those skills will be given consideration if they don't attract people who have them. You do not know if they will or won't.

e. They state they will accept applicants by mail only—*then* they put in their phone number. Why? Who knows?

f. They will accept male, female or handicapped (M/F/H).

g. They promote from within—growth opportunities!

Your approach

Step 1. Since they put in their phone number, call and ask them to send an application form.

Step. 2. Place your previous salary history, using a lead pencil, next to each of your jobs listed on your resume, neatly in the margin. (If they mail you an application this will not be necessary, since the application usually will have a space for the salary of each job listed.)

Step 3. Write your cover letter (see following example for this ad). In the second paragraph call attention to the items in your resume that meet what they want and that you have done in other jobs. "Typing @ 50 wpm + professional handling of phones and ability to accept work assignments from more than one person." *Detail* is important.

Step 4. Staple the "package" together in this order:
(Cover letter on top.)
Resume under cover letter.
Their completed application under resume.

(COVER LETTER EXAMPLE)

BAC Company
2700 Mayloo Lane, Suite 120
Middletown, U.S.A. 94362

Enclosed is my resume in reply to your advertisement for a *Clerk/Secretary.*

You will note from my resume that my past positions required heavy and accurate typing. My typing speed is 57 wpm—accurate. I am familiar with the telephone as a professional business tool and am able to handle calls in a professional manner. I have used both TWX/telex and have used word-processing equipment.

I am positive that my skills and efficiency can make a valuable contribution to your profit structure and I will look forward to discussing your position and my qualifications with you during your selection process.

Very truly yours,

Name

SAME JOB, DIFFERENT REQUIREMENTS

CLERICAL—receptionists. Must type 40+ wpm & genl. office background req'd. Call today to schedule appt. 123-1234 Linda.	CLERICAL—receptionists. Typing 40 wpm pref'd. & gen. office background desirable. Call today to schedule appt. 123-1234 Linda.

Key elements here are the words *"must"* and *"req'd."* You *must* type 40 words per minute. (Probably will have to take a test.) General office skills are *required.* If you do not type 40 plus wpm, call to ask them how firm that requirement is. You have nothing to lose, and your skill sentence may "sell" you. Do not expect too much; "must" and "required" are usually firm, but it's worth a try.

This one is wide open. They *"prefer"* someone who types 40 wpm but will consider less. They hope to find someone with a general office background by using the word *"desirable."* They probably do not pay much considering these loose statements, but the only way you will know is to go after the *offer.* Good interviewing practice, if nothing else.

Your approach

Step 1. Call Linda and read her your skill sentence and ask, "When may I come for an interview?" Allow Linda to say nothing until you're finished.

Step 2. Ask for a copy of their application to be mailed to you, if Linda asks you to send a resume. Complete the application, write a cover letter and send the cover letter, resume and completed application.

A WANT AD FOR A TOP TECHNICAL POSITION

> BIOLOGY AND IMMUNOLOGY OPPORTUNITIES
>
> A growing company, specializing in the field of biotechnology, has exciting new opportunities in the field of biotechnology for individuals with the following backgrounds.
>
> IMMUNOLOGY
>
> You must be willing to perform challenging research involving biochemistry and molecular biology as components of the immune system. Requires a B.S. plus five years experience, M.S. plus three years', or Ph.D. in immunology with some cell biology experience.
>
> CELL BIOLOGY SCIENTIST
>
> Operate and maintain a state-of-the-art cell sorter along with basic research in cell biology. A B.S. in cell biology with a background in electronic instrumentation is preferred.
> You will find our excellent compensation and benefits package very attractive. Interested applicants should mail resume, with salary history and minimum salary requirement to this paper. Ad 46578.

Anyone who qualifies *knows* exactly what this company wants. Anyone marginally qualified need not apply.

Your approach

Step 1. Write the cover letter, using the second paragraph to match your skills and education with the skills and education they seek. Do not bother with growth potential/profit statements/ and additional hype. This is a *technical* position. They are merely looking for someone to do the work—who knows *how* to do it. Just elaborate in a cover letter on what they want and on what is in your resume.

Step 2. Use a pencil and place your salary for each of your previous jobs in the margin next to the appropriate listings on your resume. Use dollar signs, decimal points and increment statements (month, year).

STOP! They have asked for a *minimum* salary requirement—not just a "salary requirement." So in paragraph three of the cover letter write the following: "Of course, salary is negotiable, but my minimum requirement would be:________." (At your technical level, you should know what salary your skills command—if not, you know what it takes to maintain or elevate your standard of living.) "HOW WILL I KNOW IF I AM TOO HIGH OR TOO LOW?" you say. You don't. If you are either, you will not hear from them. Now make paragraph four of the cover letter your closing: "I look forward to talking with you," etc.

Send the cover letter/resume to the blind ad and forget it until you hear from them. You have no choice but to wait; there's nothing else you can do to sell yourself.

SECTION THREE

THE RIGHT WAY TO CHANGE JOBS

We've given you the technique to get a job. Now we'll show you the right way to *leave* a job. Leaving a job in the right way is important because doing it correctly will help you get the *next* job. Several decades ago, having a number of short-term jobs was taboo. Now many people change jobs every two years, so it is nothing to be defensive about as long as the reasons you changed are logical.

1. REASONS WHY YOU MIGHT WANT TO CHANGE JOBS

a. You have a good job. Your supervisor is your "buddy" and is watching out for your welfare, maybe even moving you along. But if something happens to your "guardian angel," you may not be able to get along with his or her replacement. Suddenly your protector is gone and you are stuck with someone who feels threatened by your knowledge. This is terribly frustrating and can be vocationally harmful. You rebel over new policies, feel left out, react in anger and suddenly your great job becomes a nightmare.
b. The company is laying off workers. Look around before you are laid off, unless you are assured you are safe.
c. You don't *like* the job, the people you work with or anything about it, period. And you feel trapped.
d. You are being overlooked for promotions, either because of personality differences or company politics. Or you need more skills to be promoted, are doing nothing about it and the company isn't training you.

e. Your supervisor is piling his or her work on you while he or she more or less goofs off. You are infuriated, but you hang on, thinking it is a temporary situation. It turns out not to be, but your emotional state keeps you from doing anything about it, and you know you should for the sake of your sanity and your future.

Remember: *It is easier to get a job when you have a job* because when you've been unemployed, a new employer may think you have "gone stale." Besides, companies like to think they are stealing good employees away from other companies. So don't change jobs unless you have one to go to. If your new company asks why you want to change jobs, simply tell them your present position doesn't live up to the picture they painted when they hired you. Nothing more! The minute you land a new job and find out all of the duties, prepare a new resume so that you are ready for any situation.

2. HOW TO MAKE THE CHANGE

It's not hard. If you have access to a telephone, make your calls to set up appointments, using the methods we give you in this book. Set those appointments late in the day—after work is ideal. Explain to the prospective company that you are currently employed; they will go along with this. If the new company asks you to send a resume, request in your cover letter that they be discreet if they call you at work for an appointment. It's better to have them call you at home, in the evening.

3. GIVING NOTICE

When you leave the old job, *give proper notice.* Do not thumb your nose at them and walk away. You will need them as a reference later. When you get the offer, ask your new company to confirm it in writing and mail it to your home. Tell them that you must give two weeks' notice. The new company will understand this and appreciate the fact that you are acting professionally. You're worth the wait. If you are going to lose your vacation by switching from your old job, you might ask, at the time of the offer, if you could take a week's vacation, without pay if necessary, the first year. The courts have ruled that vacation-time credit begins when you're hired.

Since you may have used our methods to correct your past, rendered harmless possible bad references, covered gaps, etc., don't create a new problem by leaving an employer without giving proper notice. You are just looking for trouble all over again! Get a letter of reference too, just in case the employer resents your leaving.

You may be in for a surprise when you give your notice! You may receive a counteroffer from the firm you want to leave. If you do receive a decent counteroffer, you will have to reappraise your situation with that employer. If they do not, then you will know you made the right choice!

SECTION FOUR

ADVICE TO THE HARD-TO-EMPLOY

1. EX-OFFENDERS/WORK FURLOUGH

In many cases, the requirement for probation or parole is that you have a guarantee of a job when you get out. Despite the cooperation of some progressive businesses, this is a tough one. But our methods will help. Concentrate on how to get an interview *without* having your application or resume screened first (see "The Telephone Method for Tapping the Hidden Job Market" on pp. 159–163). Remember to work closely with your probation or parole officer. If your intention to rejoin productive society is sincere, they will be flexible. If you are no longer on probation or parole, adopt our methods as you see fit.

2. SINGLE PARENTS/DISPLACED HOMEMAKERS

Ignore the social-service labels. You are a human being with the ability to get a job if you are organized against your competition. You must survive. *Just do not tell interviewers your problems!* They will definitely think that you cannot emotionally handle a part- or full-time job.

3. SENIOR CITIZENS

Many companies will hire you, and more are doing so all the time. You have your maturity going for you—you do not have babies, rarely do you miss work for reasons associated with younger people, your skills are solid and your emotions mellowed. Employers are always complaining about young people and their lack of work ethic. A work ethic has to be learned, and you have learned it over the years. This is a selling point for you. You know how many hours you can work to supplement Social Security benefits without penalties. Remember that job-sharing is no longer an innovation. Sell your skills along with your maturity and stability and keep trying.

4. BLACK YOUTHS AND ADULTS (AND OTHER MINORITIES)

Your unemployment rate is a national tragedy! But what we advise you does not come from blindness to the reality of your problems. It comes from the results of our workshop, where we have seen you get out there and win, using methods that make you *desirable applicants* in the eyes of employers. Of course there is discrimination. There probably always will be. But the tools for job-hunting in this book make it possible for you to be competitive for a job on an equal basis with others.

If you are rejected, do not become emotional and depressed. *Keep trying.* You *will* find an employer who is not a bigot. There are thousands of employers who, if you demonstrate the right attitude at the hiring stage, indicate that you understand the necessity to make a contribution to the profit structure and are qualified in terms of training, will hire you and have no problem with your color or race. We know this because many of you who had previously received social-service employment program assistance with little or no results got jobs on your own using our methods—and not just token jobs but *good* jobs. What's more, you found out when and how to change jobs before the bottom fell out of the one you had. And everyone learned how to use the job they had to get a new and better job.

There's no instant, magic way to erase discrimination. But it can be chipped away at if you demonstrate, when applying for a job, the same confident attitude presented by nonminorities.

5. THE HANDICAPPED

There are two basic classifications of handicapped persons:

1. The visibly handicapped.

2. People whose personal problems—nervous breakdowns, work injuries, substance abuse (drugs, alcohol) and socio-economic psychological problems—have resulted in their being labeled "handicapped" for purposes of receiving social-service assistance.

The basic question here is the same for both groups: *Can* you and *will* you work at a job for 40 hours per week? If you can and will, all you have to do is make yourself attractive to employers. You *must* prove that you are capable of handling a job.

a. The visibly handicapped

Remember that you put on your application that you had "no limitations." You must believe this and come across that way in an interview. The interviewer will see your handicap and think of what special considerations you will need, if hired, for you to perform the work as normally as the person who previously held the position. *You* must stress your productivity and ability to work unassisted or without special consideration. The interviewer will almost never question your skill level but will wonder if you will cause work delays because of your handicap. In your thank-you letter after the interview underscore your ability to work unassisted or without special consideration.

b. All other handicapped

How are they going to know about your problem unless you tell them? If you follow our steps, you will come across as a desirable applicant in the eyes of a potential employer. When you do get a job, don't tell co-workers about your past problems. Keep your private life just that—private!

6. FORMER DRUG USERS

The same criteria apply as for "all other handicapped"—but don't attempt to get a job until you have recovered. You won't fool them very long, even if you succeed in getting hired, using our methods. Then there will be just another short-term, negative-reference job to contend with.

7. THE WORK-INJURED

Undoubtedly, from the date of your injury, you have found yourself involved with doctors, lawyers, state rehabilitation boards, rehabilitation counselors, etc. The original injury may have faded from your memory, and lots of people are making decisions for you. The insurance company has assigned you to a rehabilitation firm that (a) counsels you, (b) tests you to determine alternate skills, (c) sets you up in retraining schools and (d) develops jobs for you. *They* have the problem of coordinating doctors' releases to return to work, lawyers acting in your behalf and satisfying the state rehabilitation board for everyone. In working with these rehabilitation groups, we find that they can motivate you as well as coordinate all these efforts. There is only one problem, many of them admit: They have not been in private business for profit and cannot tell you how to approach employers appropriately to help yourself. Even when you are "job-developed," you still have that sense of dependency, a scar on your *mental* rehabilitation that lasts long after the physical rehabilitation is complete. When you are led to that "developed" job, you feel you got there on a crutch instead of on your own. If anything happens to that job, the process either starts all over again, if you are eligible, or because the insurance company has fulfilled all of their obligations to you and satisfied all parties, you are on your own.

This book will help you get a job on your own, but there is one roadblock: How do you transfer your skills to another job and be sure that your physical limitations, due to your injury, are not factors?

First, consider your occupation when you were injured.

Whatever you were, think of related industries that sold supplies to your trade, that provided services to your trade. Then investigate employment possibilities in those related fields, where your injury is not a factor. You already know the language of your trade and the details of the work you performed. When you complete your employment application and it asks for the reason you left your last job, place in that space "*No negative reason—will discuss in interview.*" With the professional presentation tools we have given you, this answer will not screen you out. When you are at the interview and it comes up, tell the interviewer your limitations. Do not become emotional or apologetic about them—simply say that for certain tasks you may have to ask for quick assistance, such as for lifting heavy objects (you should have help anyway). If you cannot sit or stand for too long a time or bend or stoop, etc., determine when you hear the job description whether you can do the job, and still go for the offer! This gives you more time to think about whether you can do it. If you get a job that your doctor has determined will not affect your previous injury and that you can do without physical harm, and you find that you made a mistake and tasks are expected of you that were not discussed when you were hired, use the methods we gave you in this book to *change jobs,* particularly if your employer will not make further adjustments.

Be sure to ask the employer at whose company the injury occurred not to mention the work injury to anyone checking your references. In spot-checking former supervisors of the work-injured, we have learned that some have been warned by the company not to mention "exactly" why an employee left. Most supervisors don't know how to skirt around issues. Even when they have your best interests at heart, they feel professionally honor-bound to let other "professionals" (the reference checker) know, by their tone of voice if in no other way, that something was "wrong." Their tone of voice alone could lead the reference checker to probe as deeply as possible to uncover the actual problem. Most large companies do not reveal such information, but small to large companies sometimes freely discuss all of the facts, usually in a manner hostile to you, because your injury caused them "out-of-the-ordinary daily problems." If the company you worked for is large enough to have a Personnel Department, it might be best to refer the prospective employer to the Personnel Department *only.* The odds are better that they won't say anything about it.

8. FORMER CETA WORKERS

Under the CETA program, billions of tax dollars were spent on programs designed to provide work experience or skills training or retraining to tens of thousands who were unemployed or underemployed. The success of these programs was entirely dependent on local management of the monies assigned to needy areas. Some areas slowly improved the quality of services provided with these monies, while other localities suffered at the hands of inexperienced employment management. The basic idea of CETA was good. For many, it worked. For many others, it did not. Much has been written about it, and we do not wish to rehash this program and what it may or may not have done for you if you participated in any aspect of it.

We do want to make sure that, as a former CETA worker, you do not experience future employment problems as a result of situations beyond your control.

For most of you, CETA provided two basic programs. We will list them and offer advice about how best to handle whatever involvement you may have had and what you must do to play up the positive aspect of your participation when seeking employment.

a. PSE (Public-Service Employment)

You were placed in a nonprofit setting for six to 18 months. Some of these settings were in government agency offices in your area. You might have been clerical help, a teacher's aide, a "counselor" in a people-helping agency or a child-care assistant. Others may have been assigned to do manual labor. Sometimes skills of the participants were matched to jobs as closely as possible, but in some cases, participants did nothing related to their skills. There are two things you must do if you participated in PSE:

1. List *all* of your tasks on your resume for that particular job. It may be difficult for you to imagine that what you did in CETA could be related to anything you might be seeking in a business-for-profit situation. We found that many individuals stressed the "people-helping—good-deed-doing" aspect of CETA rather than the skills they possessed or learned. Again, think of the tasks you performed from the minute you arrived at work until the minute you left. Zero in on those skills—no matter how insignificant they seemed for the work you were doing—and list them, as we instructed you to do in the section on resumes. Do not keep talking to a company's interviewer about how what you did in CETA "helped" people or furthered a "cause." The prospective employer is interested in profit-making skills, not causes. The purpose of CETA was to make you more work-ready for employment in a business for profit and to help you make that change. Even if you had an unpleasant experience in CETA (sometimes there was a "hurry up" aspect in getting people placed in government or nonprofit agencies which were not prepared fully to explore and develop the philosophy of the program), forget those experiences and concentrate on listing the skills on your resume and talking about those skills in an interview.

2. Call your former CETA program supervisor and ask him or her not to mention that you were a CETA worker. Say that CETA has received so much bad publicity that it could reflect on your ability to get work. Ask the supervisor to state instead that you worked there with "special funds" made available for a short period of time. The supervisor will be telling the truth. Then, on your application, list in

the "reason for leaving" section, "Special funding ended." You now have made an honest statement about your previous job situation without mentioning CETA.

b. Skills training

You selected a category of special schooling to learn new skills within a certain period of time. Many of you completed the required period of time in these schools and received "job development" assistance. You were "placed" in a company that agreed to take you in for "on-the-job training." The employer was reimbursed a certain amount of your salary for an established period of time. At the end of this period it was the hope of the CETA program that you would be hired permanently. If you were hired but no longer have that job, list the job on your application without mentioning that you were hired because of the CETA program. Call your former employer and ask him not to mention the circumstances under which you came to the company. List the school you attended to receive the skills training under CETA on your resume, *but do not mention that you were sent there under the CETA program.* If you do all of this, you will not be asked about CETA. If you do not do this and you *do* mention CETA, it could impair your chances for employment, depending on what the screener has read or feels about CETA.

If you were not "job-developed" after you received your skills training and did not have an on-the-job training period, merely list the schooling you received in the Education section of your resume and proceed with the previous instructions we have given you to explain employment gaps. The schooling will help you fill the gaps and give you an additional education/skills listing. Then be prepared to talk about the skills you learned during that schooling period when you get the interview. If the schooling does not apply to what you are seeking now, merely tell the interviewer you found, during schooling, that you really were not interested in that vocation after all.

9. WORKERS IN A DEPRESSED JOB MARKET AREA

We cannot improve the current job market, nor can we affect it in the future. Nothing is more frustrating than waiting for the economy to get better. There is no guarantee that your old job, or one like it, will be available again either. Unemployment benefits are bound to run out. Supplemental "laid-off" funds will dwindle and stop. You then have three choices: (a) to transfer your skills to another job or retrain in new skills for jobs that are either available or forecast to be available eventually, (b) to move to an area where jobs are more plentiful or (c) to go on welfare. Obviously, (c) is the least desirable choice both for the amount of income involved and for what it does to your self-esteem, plus its damaging side effects on you and your family.

You must survive *and* you must somehow keep working so you can be ready when you do find a job opening to which you can apply your skills. If you are in the construction industry, a machinist or in an assembly trade, look for jobs that are *related* to your former job. An inside desk sales job or an outside sales job are not beyond the realm of possibility. You need not have a fabulous wardrobe to impress vendors in blue-collar-work equipment and supplies. You will be dealing, more casually, with customers in related blue-collar firms and don't need a "corporate look." You just have to sell your skills in customer service occupations. They will teach you about their products and services. You need to have only a basic grasp of what is needed in these industries; you should have this knowledge because of your previous work with services, supplies and equipment.

If you choose to move to another area, go to a newsstand in your town that carries out-of-city or out-of-state newspapers and check the want ads. Answer some of them, either by phone or by using the presentation we gave you in this book, and see how you are received. They probably will not be willing to pay your relocation costs, and you might have to leave your family behind while you get settled in your new job.

Relocation for white-collar jobs can be investigated and handled through mid- to high-level employment agencies and relocation firms in the desired area, and this process can make the move easier.

But for blue-collar, single-skill tradespeople, the important thing is to take "some" kind of job. Naturally, it won't pay as much as you are used to. That's not the point. The point is to remain work-ready with a sense of purpose and self-esteem and not to go "stale" from sitting and slowly deteriorating. When a job market for your skill opens up, you can brag in interviews about how you kept busy, how you can jump quickly back into productive work because you did *not* sit and do nothing.

In any case, whatever you choose to do, when the job market opens up again, *use this book to make a dazzling presentation to the prospective employer* so you are heads above all those others who will be discovering that it may be necessary to *compete* for a job, not just to return to one. Remember, if you have held a job for a short or a long period and have been laid off, there's no *automatic* guarantee that you will be rehired and/or chosen over someone else without "presenting" yourself properly.

The views expressed in this book are the result of the experience gained by the staff of Job Search Workshops, Inc., through their extensive business-for-profit backgrounds, the processing of over 2,500 clients with every conceivable employment problem and their feedback from over 10,000 employment interviews and hiring process methods over a 3½-year period. We think we've honestly earned the right to give you advice on how to look for a job. We hope you take that advice and that you get not only the job you need but also the job you've always wanted. Good luck!

INDEX